MY UNCLE BARBASSOU

BY

MARIO UCHARD,

AUTHOR OF

"LA BUVEUSE DES PERLES," "LE MARIAGE DE
GERTRUDE," "FIAMETTA," ETC.

———

TRANSLATED FROM THE FRENCH BY
A. D. HALL,
ADAPTER OF "LA TOSCA," "FEDORA," "MARSA," ETC.

———

CHICAGO AND NEW YORK:
RAND, MCNALLY & COMPANY, PUBLISHERS.
1889.

My Uncle Barbassou

Mario Uchard, Arthur D. Hall

BIBLIOLIFE

MY UNCLE BARBASSOU.

CHAPTER I.

No, really, my dear Louis, I am not dead, nor ruined, nor turned pirate or monk, as you suspect in explanation of my non-appearance at your studio for the last four months. No, my wonderful inheritance has not taken wings, subtle scoffer! I am living neither on the shore of the blue waters of China, nor the red ones of Oceanica, nor the white ones of Lapland. My yacht is still in port, and does not bear me over the vasty deep. It is in vain for you, therefore, to indulge in eccentric and laborious speculations as to my uncle's will; your ironies fly wide of their mark. The will is the most astonishing thing of its kind that has ever passed through the hands of a notary, and your poor imagination could never invent such surprising adventures as those into which this stamped document has led me.

In the first place, to enable your feeble intellect to rise to the height of such a subject, I must, I confess, enlighten you a little as to "The Corsair," as you called him when you met him in Paris last winter, for only through a knowledge of his singular life can you manage to understand my adventure.

(5)

Unfortunately, there is one great difficulty. My uncle
was a very mysterious personage. He was born at Marseilles, and was left an orphan at the age of fourteen,
with a young sister, whom he brought up, and who afterward became my mother; hence his affection for me.
However, although he was my only relation, I scarcely
ever saw him except in the intervals of his sea-faring
life. Endowed with really remarkable faculties, and
with an energy which recognized no obstacle, he was one
of the best fellows in the world, as you yourself have
stated, but he was assuredly exceedingly original, from
what I know of him. I do not think that, in his adventurous career, he ever did anything like anyone else.
As you know, he died four months ago from the effects
of a sun-stroke, as he was returning from the South Pole,
at the age of sixty-three. As for the story of his life,
what I know of it is as follows:

At twenty-two, my uncle Barbassou became a Turk in
political opinions; this was under the Bourbons. His
services to the State in Turkey were never very clearly
defined in the struggles between Mehemet-Ali and the
sultan, and I don't believe he understood them very well
himself, for he served the two princes alternately with
equal bravery and equal sincerity. By chance, he happened
to be with Ibrahim, when the latter defied the Turks at the
battle of Konieh; but, carried too far in that famous
charge which he commanded and which decided the victory, my poor uncle had the misfortune to fall wounded
into the hands of the vanquished. A prisoner of Kur-
chid-Pacha, and soon cured of his wound, he expected
to be executed, when, to his great joy, his punishment
was commuted to the galleys. There he remained for
three years without succeeding in escaping, until one

fine day he found himself in the hands of the sultan, who appointed him pacha, giving him a command in the war in Syria. What circumstance put an end to his political career, and how he obtained from the Pope his title of Count of the Holy Empire, no one knows.

What is certain is that, weary of grandeur, Barbassou-Pacha returned and established himself, two years ago, in Provence, whence he departed one morning for Africa in a ship which he had purchased at Toulon. He then engaged in the spice trade. It was at the end of one of these voyages that he published his celebrated ontologi-cal pamphlet on the negro races, a pamphlet which created a great stir and was highly praised by the Acad-·emy. The principal events of his Odyssey known, the particular actions and doings of Barbassou-Pacha are lost in conjecture. Physically, you can probably recall the Marseillaise—six feet tall, of thin frame, but with muscles of steel; you can remember still that formid-able, bearded face, that fierce eye, that harsh voice—in fact, that type of a retired pirate, as you laughingly said. However, he was very easy to get along with, and the best of uncles.

Personally, as far back as I can remember, this is all that I have ever known of him. As he was always at sea, he sent me to school at a very early age. One year, when he was at the chateau de Férouzat, he sent for me during the vacation. I was six years old, and I saw him then for the first time. He raised me in his arms, and exam-ined my face and profile; then, turning me gently round and round in the air, he scrutinized my figure, after which, apparently satisfied, he placed me on the ground with infinite precaution, as if afraid of breaking me,

"Kiss your aunt," he said to me,

I obeyed.

My aunt was then a very handsome woman, twenty-two or twenty-three years old; a brunette, with great, black, almond-shaped eyes, and a perfectly oval face. She took me in her lap and covered me with kisses, lavishing upon me the tenderest names, mingled with words in a foreign tongue, which seemed like music, her voice was so sweet and melodious. I took a great fancy to her. My uncle let me do just as I liked and never placed any obstacle in the way of my wishes. So that, at the end of vacation, I did not want to return to school, and should certainly have succeeded in my desire if Barbassou-Pacha's ship had not been waiting for him at Toulon.

You can imagine with what joy I returned to Férouzat the following year. My uncle received me with the same kindness and subjected me to the same examination. His solicitude quieted, he said: " Kiss your aunt."

I kissed my aunt, but, while doing so, I was a little astonished at finding her very much changed. She had become a blonde, with a pink and white complexion. A certain tendency to stoutness, which was marvelously becoming to her, gave her the appearance of a girl of eighteen. More timid than at our first interview, she proferred me her rosy cheek with a blush. I remarked also that she had modified her accent, which resembled very much that of one of my school comrades who was a Hollander. As I expressed my surprise at this change, my uncle informed me that they had just come from Java. This explanation was sufficient for me and I asked no more questions, and from that time I became accustomed to the different metamorphoses my aunt underwent each year. The transformation which pleased me the least was the one she contracted in consequence of a voyage to Bourbon, from whence she returned a mulattress, but without ceasing, however, to be remarkably pretty. My uncle, besides, was always charming to her, and I never knew a happier couple. Once, unfortunately, engaged in a heavy business enterprise, Barbassou-Pacha remained absent three years, and when I came again to Férouzat, I found him quite alone. I asked after my aunt; he was a widower. As this accident did not appear to affect him much, I took my cue from him and followed his example.

Since that time I have never seen a woman at the chateau, except once, in a lonely part of the park, where I encountered two mysterious figures carefully veiled. They were walking, accompanied by an old man of singular appearance, clothed in a long robe, and with a turban on his head. My uncle told me that it was His Excellency, Mohammed-Aziz, one of his friends from Constantinople, whom he had received with his family on account of his persecution by the sultan; he had lodged him in another little chateau adjoining Férouzat, in order that they might live more conveniently in the Turkish fashion; the young persons were two of his daughters.

After that year, I scarcely ever visited Provence; my uncle staid in China and Japan for five years without returning, and my only relations with him were through his banker at Paris, with whom he had opened for me an unlimited credit, which I took advantage of to the fullest extent, and spent my money in the most foolish manner.

You know how, a few months ago, I received the letter which announced to me an unexpected misfortune, and

demanded my immediate presence at Férouzat for the
opening of the will; my poor uncle had died in Abyssinia.

The day after my arrival here I was scarcely up when
Féraudet, the notary, was announced. He entered with
an armful of papers. I would have preferred not to act
like a man greedy for his inheritance, and to have put off
material affairs for a few days; but the notary said to me
that there were certain clauses in the will which neces-
sitated a prompt examination. My uncle left me numerous charges and legacies for the benefit of certain distant
relations. All this was told me with the mournful tone
befitting the circumstances, and at the same time with
the air of a man who felt that he was the bearer of an
extraordinary document and was preparing its effect.
Finally, he opened the will; it was drawn up as follows:

"Chateau de Férouzat, ——, 18—.

"I, the undersigned, Claude Anatole Gratien Barbassou, Count of Monteclaro, do hereby declare and appoint
as universal legatee and sole heir of my property, real
and personal, my nephew, Jérôme André de Peyrade, son
of my sister, and I hereby charge the aforesaid with the
fulfillment of the following bequests:

"1. To my well-beloved wife and legitimate spouse,
Lia Rachel Euphroisine Ben Lévy, milliner at Constantinople, and living there in the Fauborg of Péra:
1st, the sum of four thousand five hundred francs,
due to her by our marriage contract; 2d, my house at
Péra, which she inhabits, including all the appurtenances
thereto; 3d, the sum of twelve thousand francs to be
divided as she wishes among our various children.

"*Item*, To my well-beloved wife and legitimate spouse,

Sophia Eudoxia, Countess of Monteclaro (*née* de Cornalis), living at Corfu: 1st, the sum of five hundred thousand francs, due to her by our marriage contract; 2d, the clock and vases of Dresden china which are upon my mantlepiece; 3d, the Virgin, by Perugini, which is in my *salon* at Férouzat.

"*Item*. To my well-beloved wife and legitimate spouse, Marie Gretchen van Cloth, living at Amsterdam: 1st, the sum of twenty thousand francs, due to her by our marriage contract; 2d, the sum of sixty thousand francs to be divided as she wishes among our various children; 3d, my table-service of Dutch Faience, No. 3; 4th, a music-box playing four symphonies by Haydn.

"*Item*. To my well-beloved wife and legitimate spouse, Marie Louise Antoinette Cora de La Pescade, living at the Grands-Palmiers (Isle of Bourbon), my plantation, where she now resides, including the dependencies of the Grand Morne.

"*Item*. To my well-beloved wife and legitimate spouse, Anita Josepha Christina de Postero, living at Cadiz: 1st, the sum of twelve thousand francs, due to her by our marriage contract; 2d, my pardon for her adventure with my lieutenant, Jean Bonaffé."

If any strict person should criticise the conjugal principles of my uncle, I would answer him that Barbassou-Pacha was a Turk and Mohammedan, that, consequently, he is deserving only of praise for faithfully obeying the laws of the prophet which permitted him such a wealth of wives, without in the least overstepping the limits of propriety, and that he had, on the contrary, in this respect, piously fulfilled a religious duty, which, according to all appearance, his premature death alone had prevented him from accomplishing with more fervor. I hope that Allah will take into account at least his efforts.

This is said for the sake of a memory which is dear to me, and the principal clauses of the will announced, I add that, the matrimonial legacies of my uncle deducted, there remained to me about thirty-seven millions.

"So much for the legal provisions, monsieur," continued the notary, when he had finished his reading. "I have now to give you a sealed letter which your uncle confided to me to deliver to you alone after his death. I was ordered to destroy it without opening it, in case your death should precede his. I am, therefore, ignorant of the contents which must be read only by you. Will you, if you please, sign this receipt stating that the seals are intact, and that I have given the letter into your hands."

He presented me with a paper, which I read and signed.

"Is that all?" I asked.

"Not yet, monsieur," he replied, drawing from his pocket another envelope. "Here is a document, also sealed, which was addressed to me. I was to open it only in case your uncle's will should be null and void— your death having preceded his. This document, he told me, was, in that case, to regulate the disposition of his property. Your existence being duly established, my written and formal orders enjoin me to burn before your eyes this paper, which is now of no use."

He then made me examine the seals, and taking from my bureau a candle, he lighted it and burned the document, the contents of which will never be known. This formality accomplished, he took his departure.

Left alone, I sat down to read the letter which the notary had left with me. I divined some mystery, and I had a vague presentiment that the letter would contain the decree of my future destiny. These last words from my uncle, which seemed to me to come from the tomb, revived in my heart the deepest regrets for his death. I finally tore open the envelope with a trembling hand.

These are its contents:

"MY DEAR CHILD: When you read this, I shall have finished my earthly career. Do me the kindness not to grieve too much, and to be a man. You know my ideas in regard to death. I have never looked upon it as a misfortune, convinced that it is simply a transition to a higher sphere. Follow the same line of reasoning and do not weep for me like a child. I have lived; it is now your turn! I wish your old friend to be only a pleasant memory to you. Think of him in your happiness and imagine that he shares it.

"Now to business.

"I leave you all my property, in order to avoid complications; my will is properly drawn up, and you can enter at once into possession without more formality. However, there is one last request, which I am sure your heart will counsel you to fulfill. I have a god-daughter who has always shared with you my affection. If I have kept her existence a secret from you, it was because circumstances might arise which would render the revelation I now make, useless. She is an orphan, she will soon be seventeen, and I confide her to your care. Her name is Anna Campbell, she is in Paris at the Convent des Oiseaux, where she is finishing her education. She has no relations except an aunt, her mother's sister;

Madame Saulnier, who lives at No. 20 Rue Barbet de Jouy. You have only to present yourself to this lady and tell her your name. She knows that I have appointed you as the guardian of my ward; that you are the one who will replace me. She knows, in fact, *all my intentions.*

"I underline these words, for they represent my dearest hopes. I have brought up Anna with the hope of giving her to you as a wife, and of thus sharing my fortune between you, relying upon you to carry out my wishes. Whether marriage is or is not a matter of great consequence for a man, it is the most important event in a woman's life. With you, I know that I need not fear my little girl will be unhappy. If I do not return from this voyage, you will have plenty of time to continue your bachelor's life; but I count upon your friendship to render me this little service of marrying her when the time comes. I think that you will do well to wait two or three years. She is still a trifle thin, but I assure you her mother was a fine woman. You will find both their pictures together in one of the medallions in the drawer of my secretary. (Don't make a mistake; it is the one numbered 13.)

"Now that the affair is settled, I have only a few more words to say to you. If Féraudet has followed my instructions, as I suppose he has, he must have burnt a paper in your presence. It was a second will which made my god-daughter, Anna Campbell, sole legatee of all my property, if you had not been living. Now that all is in order, and you have survived me, you understand that I have not wished to complicate matters by forcing you to submit to the formalities and chicaneries which a minor, inheriting with you, would have given rise to; you would have had endless trouble. However, we

must take precautions in case some accident should
befall you before your marriage with Anna. Heaven
knows what would become of the property then! As I
desire that my money should go to my children, I beg
you not to fail to make a will in favor of Anna, so that
all may go to her, without legal trouble. I trust in you
for this. You will find her full name and all directions
in the first page of my private ledger, where is set down
the credit opened for her, as well as for you, at my
banker's, and which formed a special account for you
both. Madame Saulnier is in the habit of drawing what
she needs; till your marriage, take care of this; make
her credit good.

"This arranged, my boy, go on your own way. I need
not ask you, I know, to think sometimes of your old
uncle; I know your character, that is enough for me.
On my side, I thank you for what you have been to
me, and I give you my blessing from the bottom of my
heart.

"Now, great baby, don't break down; I am in heaven,
my soul is free and rejoices in the splendor of the infinite.
Is there anything in that to grieve at? Farewell."

After reading this letter, my dear Louis, need I tell
you that I did exactly the contrary to what my poor
uncle had ordered me, and broke down? Tears rolled
down my cheeks, and I could no longer see the word
"Farewell" which I pressed to my lips.

His tenderness, his touching anxiety to console my
grief, his boundless confidence in my affection, my loyalty—I was overcome with sorrow, but I was glad to feel
myself worthy the great heart of that man who had
loaded me with benefits with the affection of a father. It
seemed to me that I had never loved him enough, and the

grief at his loss was mingled with something like remorse.
I swore to him to fulfill his requests, as if he could
hear me; at the bottom of my heart, besides, I was sure
he was looking down on me.

When my tears were dried, I did not delay in pro-
ceeding to accomplish his last commands. I hastened to
his chamber, opened his secretary, and found the portraits.
One, a miniature, representing a woman of twenty-five,
the other a photograph of Anna Campbell at fifteen; not
so pretty as her mother, perhaps, still she has a charming,
child-like face. The poor little thing was doubtless tired
sitting for her picture, for the expression is somewhat
pouting and unnatural. She promises, however, to be
beautiful, when she has passed the awkward age. I felt a
sudden sentiment of affection for the unknown girl whose
guardian I am, and whose husband I am to be. Upon
her cold likeness, I renewed my vow to my uncle to obey
his wishes; then, taking a pen, I made a will instituting
Anna Campbell universal legatee of all the property my
uncle had left us.

But, one part of my inheritance, the strangest and
most unexpected of all, was still unknown to both the
notary and myself.

———

CHAPTER II.

I do not wish to make myself out better than I am;
yet, I assure you, my dear Louis, that, despite the quite
natural excitement I felt at being master of such a fortune,
when I had finished with the legal business, my first
thought was to pay the memory of my poor uncle a
tribute of mourning and regret. I would have consid-

ered it ungrateful and impious to be in too great a haste to enjoy the wealth of such a benefactor. His loss really left a cruel void in my heart; I decided then to live at least some months at Férouzat. I wrote immediately to Anna Campbell's aunt telling her my resolution to fulfill the wishes of my second father, and begging her to dispose of me in all things, as a protector and a friend ready to answer any appeal. Four days after, I received· from her a most cordial and well expressed letter. She assured me of her confidence in all the good my uncle had said of me; she gave me news of my fiancée, "who, although as yet only a child, promises already to be an accomplished woman."

These duties acquitted, I installed myself in my retreat, and set to work.

I was obliged to examine all that my uncle had bequeathed me, and heaven only knows what was contained in the chateau de Férouzat! Every day I made some new discovery in the rooms filled with rare furniture and ornaments of all ages and all countries; Barbassou-Pacha was a great collector, and there were quantities of trunks and drawers filled with rare stuffs, costumes, and objects of art; my steward, himself, did not know half what there was in the house.

But the most charming and most wonderful thing of all my inheritance was Kasre-el-Nouzha, my neighboring property. Kasre-el-Nouzha is a Turkish fancy of my uncle's. These three Arabic words may be translated into Spanish by *Buen-Retiro*, literally "Castle of Pleas- . ure." It is only separated from Férouzat by a wall, and is the place once inhabited by the exiled minister who fled from the persecutions of the sultan. Imagine, hidden behind the leafy trees of a great park, a delicious

2

palace of the purest Oriental architecture, a sort of temple transplanted from Asia. My uncle Barbassou planned it after one of the residences of the King of Cashmere. Inside of Kasre, you might believe yourself in the house of some lord of Stamboul or Bagdad. The rooms are spacious, the ornamentation and the furniture most luxurious, everything is studied with the care of an artist and the exactitude of an archæologist, European comfort charmingly mingled with Turkish simplicity. It is a perfect masterpiece, the palace of a pacha dropped from the skies upon the soil of Provence. A little door in the wall of the park opens into this oasis. You can imagine whether I passed long hours there dreaming of the Thousand and One Nights.

I did not, however, neglect my work, for you do not suppose, I imagine, that my princely fortune would ever make me desert science. In the midst of my numerous follies, and despite the temptations of the life I have led up to my present age of twenty-six, I have always preserved that love of study which gives so many happy hours, in the forced respite from worldly pleasures, to every man of intelligence. The polytechnic school and the pursuit of the x, which my uncle imposed upon me, have developed in me examining instincts. I have ended with a certain taste for transcendental ideas. I will acknowledge to you that I class in the rank of Mollusks, the man, who, of his own free will, is contented to eat, drink, and sleep, without doing any brain-work or cultivating his intellect. That is why you call me the *savant*. I went to work on my book, therefore, with real ardor, and my essay on the origin of sensation had made good progress when the great event happened which I have undertaken to narrate to you.

I had been living in this solitary manner for two weeks, when, one evening, on my return from Arles, where I had been for a couple of days on business, I learned that His Excellency, Mohammed-Aziz, the old friend of my uncle, whom I remembered having seen once, had arrived the previous evening at the chateau, ignorant of Barbassou Pacha's death. I confess that I was not particularly overjoyed at this piece of news; but, in memory of the dear departed, I could not refuse the expected hospitality. They told me that His Excellency had gone at once to install himself at Kasre-el-Nouzha, where it had been his custom to live. I sent a messenger to bid him welcome, and to ask him to inform me if he would allow me to call upon him. He answered that he was at my orders and that he awaited me. I departed at once to pay him a visit.

I found Mohammed-Aziz upon the threshold, grave and sad; he received me with a salute, the respect of which embarrassed me a little, coming from a man of his age. He led me into the *salon*, in the four corners of which murmured fountains of perfumed water, falling into little basins of alabaster, ornamented with flowers. He made me sit down on the silken divan, which, very deep, very low, and covered with cushions, extended all around the four sides of the apartment. Once seated, I addressed to him a few words of condolence; he answered me in Turkish. The interview was becoming somewhat difficult; but, seeing that I did not understand him, he commenced with an accent which I can not describe.

"*Povera excellenza Barbassou-Pacha! finito-morto!*"

I answered him in Italian; he understood me fairly well. We were saved.

I then related to him the misfortune which had caused
my uncle's death. He listened to me with an appearance of the greatest affliction.

"*Dunque*," he said, anxiously, "*voi signor padrono?
Voi heritare di tutto? ordinare? commandare?*"

"Believe me, Your Excellency," I replied, "nothing
will be changed here, as far as you are concerned, by my
uncle's death, and I shall do my best to be his second self."

He appeared satisfied, and sighed like a man relieved
of a great weight. After a moment, he asked me if I
would allow him to make me acquainted with his household.

"I shall be enchanted, Your Excellency, if you will
present me to your family."

He went to the door and clapped his hands.

I expected, according to Mussulman customs, to see
the wives or the daughters of my guest appear enveloped in
their triple veils. I could not restrain a cry of surprise
when I saw four young girls enter, clothed in the exquisite Oriental costume, their faces uncovered, and all four
so young, beautiful, and graceful, that I was for an
instant dazzled. I thought they were his daughters.

Hesitating and timid, they paused a few steps from
us. In my amazement, I sought in vain for something
to say to them, when, in obedience to a few words from
their father, they came to me one after the other, and
with a wild, shy grace, indescribably charming, each one
of them, bending her head, placed her hand on her
forehead, raised my hand and kissed it.

I must confess that I entirely lost my head. I don't
know what I faltered out. I think that I assured them
that they and their father would find in me, in place of
my uncle, a venerable and devoted friend; but, as they did

not understand a word of French, my eloquence was lost. They at once seated themselves upon the divan, and I thought of nothing except how to prolong my visit. Mohammed told me their charming names. They were called · Kondjé-Gul, Hadidjé, Nazli, and Zouhra. When, like a proud father, he praised their beauty, I joined in with him, and very certainly my enthusiasm flattered him.

They were all four possessed of such wonderful, and, at the same time, such a different style of beauty that they looked as if purposely grouped together to form the most exquisite of pictures; great, black eyes, soft, shy, and languishing as those of the gazelle, with that Eastern expression which we never see; smiling lips, disclosing pearly teeth; complexions, protected by the veil from the sun's rays, which seemed really formed of lilies and roses, to use a time-honored expression. In their rich robes of gauze and silk of the most harmonious colors, their poses and movements had a certain feline suppleness and exotic grace which one must have seen in Mussulman maidens to fully understand its voluptuous languor. It seemed to me that I was playing a part in some Arabian story, and my brain was filled with the most foolish imaginings.

While, through courtesy, I tried my best to converse with their father, gaining confidence little by little, they commenced to whisper among themselves, and every once in a while a little silvery mischievous laugh was heard. I spoke to them gaily, shaking my finger at them, and they answered with renewed laughter, so that, at the end of half an hour, we felt quite at home with one another. We talked by means of gestures, and our eyes rendered almost superfluous the laborious intervention of Mohammed as interpreter. He appeared, moreover, delighted at seeing us become so well acquainted.

To teach them my name, I pronounced several times the word André. They understood and made me, in their turn, speak their names. My attempts at Hadidjé created great laughter, because of the difficulty I had in articulating the guttural aspirate. Seeing that I could not manage it, she took me by both hands, her face almost touching mine. " Hadidjé!" she cried. And I repeated "Hadidjé!" It was absurd but delightful. I had to go through the same lesson with each of them, but the pleasantest of all was when Kondjé-Gul took her turn. By some accident she let fall a word of Italian. I addressed her in that language; she knew it a little. You can imagine my joy. We immediately asked each other a multitude of questions. Her sisters looked at us, opening wide their great eyes.

At this moment a Greek servant entered, followed by two women bearing dinner upon plates which they deposited upon low tables of ebony inlaid with mother-of-pearl. Discretion commanded me to take my departure after a very long visit, and I prepared to do so. Immediately there arose a chorus of confused words from my young friends which I took to mean regret at my going. His Excellency happily intervened by inviting me to dinner. Need I say that I accepted?

I sat down like them upon the carpet, with my legs crossed, and we commenced a delicious repast. Champagne was brought for me, an attention of which I was fully sensible. I was seated beside Nazli with Kondjé-Gul on my left, and Hadidjé and Zouhra opposite. I will not tell you what dishes were served; my thoughts were elsewhere.

" How old are you?" asked Kondjé-Gul.

" Twenty-six," I answered, " and you?"

" I shall soon be eighteen."

She then told me the age of the others. Hadidjé was
the eldest, being nineteen; Nazli and Zouhra between
seventeen and eighteen. Our gaiety and their chatter
never stopped. As they drank only water, I thought-
lessly said to Kondjé-Gul:

" Won't you taste the wine of France?"

At this proposition she looked so alarmed that the
others asked her to translate my words. Then ensued great agitation, followed by a discussion in which
their father took part. I was afraid I had offended
them, when His Excellency finally said a few words which
seemed decisive. Then, with a bright blush and with
the most graceful hesitation, Kondjé-Gul took my glass
and drank, at first with a charming little grimace, then
with such an air of satisfaction that we all burst out
laughing.

When I saw her touch my glass, I confess, I felt my
heart beat as if her lips had touched mine in a kiss.
Judge of my feelings when Zouhra, Nazli, and Hadidjé
all held out their hands to take my glass. They drank
all round, and I after them. Their abandon mingled with
modest reserve, the timidity which they had conquered,
for fear, doubtless, of wounding me by refusing what they
thought to be in conformity with our French customs, all
this touched me, delighted me, even intimidated me at
times so that I could scarcely meet their looks. At
the end of the repast, the same Greek servants cleared
the tables. It was now dark, and the candles in the
chandeliers were lighted. Through the closed Persian
blinds was wafted the perfume of myrtle and lilac

Cigarettes were brought. Zouhra took one, lit it, and
after a few puffs, offered it to me.

Tell me, Louis, can you imagine your friend softly
reclining upon a pile of cushions? About him, four
houris from the paradise of Mahomet, in their exquisite
sultana costumes, laughing and chattering; all four so
beautiful that, had I been Paris, I could not have decided
to whom to give the apple. I repeat to you, I had to
make a great effort to convince myself that it was all real.
After some time, I perceived that Mohammed-Aziz was
no longer there; but thanks to Kondjé-Gul, my interpreter,
our conversation became active and general. Hadidjé
taught me a Turkish game which is played with flowers,
but which I can not describe to you, as I did not understand it.

To tell you how that evening passed, would be to relate
a dazzling dream of enchantment. I showed them, in
my turn, a French game. You know it. A ribbon is
knotted at both ends, and all hold it, seated on the ground
in a circle. On the ribbon is a ring, which must be seized
by one of the players. What laughter and fun it created! Each of them naturally chose me as their mark,
and imprisoned me in their soft white arms in their efforts
to obtain the ring.

It was almost midnight when His Excellency returned.
I had lost all consciousness of time; but now I must
depart. While I was preparing to do so and as I was
saying a few words to Kondjé-Gul, Mohammed-Aziz
spoke to Zouhra, Nazli, and Hadidjé. It seemed to me
that he questioned them and they answered in the negative. Then he spoke longer to Kondjé-Gul; he seemed
to me to be demanding an account of my conversation
with her and to be dissatisfied at the result. I thought,

with annoyance, that perhaps I had caused her to be reprimanded. Finally, he doubtless ordered them to retire; for they came to me one after the other and as at their entrance, each of them bowed respectfully, placing her fingers on her forehead, and kissed my hand; after which they left the room, leaving me in a state of bewilderment impossible to describe.

I was about to make some apology to Mohammed, for I was afraid that he would place obstacles in the way of my enjoying similar evenings, when he said to me with an anxious air, in his idiom which I will not attempt to reproduce:

"May I hope that the signor is satisfied?"

"What, Your Excellency?" I cried, seizing both his hands. "I am delighted. And you can not give me greater pleasure than in treating me exactly as you would my uncle."

"They have not displeased your lordship!" he continued.

"Your daughters? They are adorable. And my only fear is that they may not share the kindly feeling with which they have inspired me."

"Ah! Then it is not because your lordship is displeased that Your Excellency has not spoken his wishes to any of them."

"My wishes? What wishes could I express to any of them?"

"Since they belong to your lordship," he responded.

"They belong to me? Who?"

"Why, Kondjé-Gul, Zouhra, Hadidjé, Nazli."

"They belong to me?" I cried, utterly amazed and stupefied.

"Certainly," said Mohammed, as astonished as I,

"His Excellency, Barbassou-Pacha, whose eunuch I had
the honor to be, ordered me to purchase him four slaves
for his harem. As he is dead, and your lordship
replaces him as master, I had supposed——"

"Ah!!!"

I will not attempt to express to you the meaning of
the cry which escaped me. You can imagine all the
sentiments it contained. In fact, I thought this time
that I had certainly gone mad, or was dreaming of the
Thousand and One Nights. This original and sumptuous
palace was a harem, and this harem was mine! These
four scheherezades, whose beauty and fascinating graces
had made such an impression on me, were my slaves,
and waited only a sign from me!

Mohammed, incapable of understanding my agitation,
regarded me with a piteous, frightened air, as if he
feared some disgrace.

"It is well," said I. "Leave me."

He obeyed, saluted me without speaking, and departed.

As soon as I was alone, with nothing to restrain me,
I ran about the *salon* like a madman, and gave free reins
to my joy. I snatched from the carpet a ribbon forgotten
by Kondjé-Gul and pressed it passionately to my lips,
and then the scattered flowers with which Hadidjé and
Zouhra had played.

Louis, you do not expect me, I hope, to analyze all
the remarkable emotions through which I passed at that
moment. What had happened to me seemed almost
supernatural, and I do not know what legend, novel, or
romance has ever touched upon a situation so surprising
as that of which I was the hero. Certain rigid people
who offer their daughters the Arabian Nights to read,
filled with the escapades and love adventures of the

Caliph of Bagdad, would consider such a romance very bold, only because the scene is not laid in Persia or Samarcand. However, my story is identical, and the most modest maiden would read it without a blush if I were called Hassan instead of André.

You understand now, my dear Louis, how the complications of my uncle's will have prevented me from writing to you for over four months. I will relate to you hereafter the incidents of this remarkable situation, this quadruple love of which I am possessed, and I will keep you informed of all that takes place. Say, if you like, in the commonplace sphere of your limited sensations, that all this is madness. I love, I adore, like a poet, like a heathen, as you choose; but you see, my uncle, who was a Mussulman, left me a harem—what could I do?

If your work leaves you any leisure, *don't* come to Férouzat. We sultans wish to be alone.

I need not advise you, I suppose, to keep this letter carefully concealed from your wife.

CHAPTER III.

Madame, I will tell you the truth. Yes, I am of a susceptible disposition, more so perhaps than most Provençals. I acknowledge it, and I do not blush at it; but I am also, deign to believe me, a lover of the proprieties, and it would be with great regret that I should see myself fall in your esteem. Now, from some words of delicate raillery, hidden like little serpents among the condolences of your mischievous letter, I already understood that, with a lack of all delicacy, and at the risk of covering me with confusion, that miserable Louis had played me

an outrageous trick by reading to you the follies I wrote
him last week. Do not deny it! He shamelessly con-
fesses it to-day in his letter to me, adding even that you
laughed. Great heavens! What must you have thought
of me? After such an adventure, I should never dare
to face you again if I could not excuse myself by declaring at once that the whole story is only a mystification,
imagined as an answer to his impertinent jests in regard
to my uncle Barbassou's will. Louis allowed himself to
be caught in the trap like a simpleton. To have you
believe it also, would make me die of shame.

Madame, I prefer to avow all. I am not at all the
hero of a sultanic romance. I am a good young man, a
friend of morality and decorum, although you have often
honored me with the title of "downright odd character."
Please to consider, also, that I have been culpable only
through too much ingenuity. I did not suppose that
Louis would show you that extravagant letter, for I
expressly recommended him to hide it from you. My only
fault in all this would be, therefore, having forgotten
that a woman of your intelligence may read everything,
when she has the heart and the husband that you
have.

In fact, madame, I do not know why I should excuse
myself so persistently; I perceive that through my apolo-
gies I run great risk of aggravating my fault. What have
I written, after all, except a sorry re-hash of one of
those Arabian tales, which on winter evenings you have
often read to young girls before the eyes of their
delighted mothers? In thinking it over, I understand now
that if you laughed, it was surely at the poverty of my
imagination. You recalled the golden palace, and the
hundred wives of the Caliph Haroun al Raschid; but

please consider also that I am a poor Provençal, and not a sultan.

"*Mes voeux sont ceux d'un simple bachelier.*"

Notice, besides, that through a respect for probability, as well as local color, I have limited myself to a very simple harem in point of numbers. Like those authors who end by falling seriously in love with the heroines they invent, I am so fascinated with the creatures of my dream that to enjoy the charm of illusion, I have not wished to surpass the limits of a possible romance.

But since I have allowed myself to fall into such folly do you not think, on reflection, that it would be a pity to abandon such a romance at the very first pages? Is it not surprising that no novelist has ever conceived a similar plot? Would it not be at once a work for a moralist and for a philosopher, worthy both of a poet and a scholar? Our poor world, madame, moves in such a narrow circle of limited sensations and passions that it seems to me that every thoughtful mind must at times find itself restricted. What happiness, with a flight of the imagination, to escape from that prison which prejudice erects and keeps bolted! To spread one's wings into the regions of dreamland! A slave of our civilized conventionalities to wander at liberty through the shadowy paths of the heathen world, peopled with fascinating, laughing nymphs   Like a happy son of Asia's skies to meander through gardens of sycamores and make love to sultanas! The Bois de Boulogne is doubtless a charming place, madame, but confess that it is inferior to the Valley of Roses, and that the painted damsels one meets there pale before my almehs.

What! must I be blamed for my thirst for the ideal? Do you not think, you who are a reader of novels, that

on the contrary it would be instructive as well as interesting to study the odd incidents which would naturally
result from a story of Oriental love in the heart of
France? What unexpected contrasts and events! Is not
the absence of such a study a hiatus in our very remarkable literature?

But I see upon your lips a word which freezes me—
"Immoral! Immoral!"

Madame, that word shows me that you strangely
misinterpret my pure intentions. You are a woman of
too much intelligence; you should not do that. Let us
have an explanation as philosophers; as moralists. Suppose that I were called Hassan; you would then certainly read without a frown the story of my imaginary
loves, and, if there were any sad incidents, you would
accord them, perhaps, the tribute of the tears which you
have doubtless shed over the sorrows of poor Namouna.
The question of morality is certainly then only a question of latitude, and the eccentricity of my situation
would disappear at once if I lived on the banks of the
Bosporus or inhabited some palace of Bagdad.

Would you pause at the higher question of sentiment?
It is precisely that psychological point of view that I
propose to treat, madame. Were it only to seek to discover if the human soul, freed from all pressure, is susceptible of expanding in the infinite like gas; to mingle
positive and material science with ethereal sensualism,
such is my end. A simple love, we know what that is,
but to adore four women at once, although so many
honest people think it quite sufficient to love but one,
seems to me a praiseworthy attempt, worthy of inflaming
the heart of a poet as well as the brain of a scholar seeking the vital fluid and the sources of sensation. Such a

study, although assuredly arduous and severe, would not be without glory you must acknowledge, if, peradventure, it should end logically in the triumph of sublime Christian love over pagan or Mohammedan polygamy.

Beside, madame, in reproaching me with my little harem, would you speak ill of King David, or of Solomon with his seven hundred wives? Without reverting to the biblical legends of those venerated sovereigns, have you not read the classics? In what, I beg you, is the poem of Don Juan more moral than my subject? Did good La Fontaine lose anything of his puremindedness by dipping his pen in the ink of Boccaccio? The morality of a book, madame, lies in the morality of the author, who first respects himself by respecting his public, and who does not lead his readers into bad company for the sake of inculcating them with bad sentiments. It pleases me to paint a picture of those ideal loves which every romantic youth of twenty must have dreamt of; to replace courtesans and vice by grace and purity, and like those charming heathen poets, who have so delighted us, to mingle the anacreontic with the idyllic. Open the first novel you come across, madame, and I will give up my harem if you do not find that the interest turns upon an infringement of the seventh commandment, in thought, in action. The same minotaur serves us since the days of Menelaus. The seventh commandment, always the seventh commandment; it is inevitable as well as monotonous.

Do you prefer the fashionable romances of the lives of the demi-monde? Those revelations where all is impure, venal, degrading! I pause, madame, out of respect for you as well as for my pen.

Do you like better, perchance, those studies of moral-

ists upon " Woman," where, on the first page, the author
warns his readers that he "speaks only for chaste ears."
Madame, it is my boast never to write a line that an honest woman may not read. My book will certainly lose
thereby a large sale, but I shall console myself with the
thought that if I cause sometimes upon your lips a smile,
that smile, at least, will never be accompanied by a blush.
Nephew of a pacha, it seemed to me novel to lay the
scene of a Turkish romance in Provence, and to write
thus a psychological essay. Love is necessary in every
romance. Am I to blame, then, if the habits of the
Orient admit of a different way of loving from our own?
Acknowledge, moreover, that my heroines are more
poetic than those fashionable damsels, whom I, like
any other author, had a right to make my hero fall in
love with. To excuse myself, I shall say, like the artless
Chamfort: " Is it my fault if I love better the women
I love, than those I do not love?"

P. S.—Above all, not a word to Louis of the mystification I have made him the victim of.

———

CHAPTER IV.

You idiot, you have gotten me into a horrible scrape!
What! I confide to you the astonishing position in which
I am placed, impressing upon you the most absolute
secrecy, and you coolly show my letter to your wife, at
the risk of exposing me, by your indiscretion, to the
most pungent jests and sarcasms. Did not you understand that, if my adventure became noised about, Paris
would be too hot to hold me; that I should be the butt
of all the newspapers as an eccentric personage; that I

could no longer appear at the club, at the theatre, or in a drawing-room without being received with jeering smiles or looks of amazement and curiosity? I can imagine myself in the Bois, followed by loungers delighted at seeing "the gentleman who owns a harem." Have you lost all intelligence, to treat me with such abominable treachery?

I insist upon your repairing your folly by accepting, in the eyes of your wife, my version of the story; that it was all a fabrication, for I have written her that not a word of it was true; that it is a romance I invented to occupy my leisure moments during the time I am forced to remain in solitude at Férouzat in order to wind up the business connected with my inheritance. In short, as I have no doubt she will not delay in showing you also my letter to her, I exact of your friendship that you feign to believe it. On this condition alone, will I continue to give you my confidence, and I shall suspend it till you have written me and given me your solemn word of honor not to betray it again.

CHAPTER V.

I have your promise, and I take up my story at the point I left off. You will see what you have lost. Only one word to begin with.

My friend, I am relating to you a very extraordinary story, especially as regards the unknown sensations I experience at every step, for my love affairs, you see, do not resemble those of any other lover, and it would be a great loss for the future of psychology if the hero of such an adventure were not, like myself, a philosopher capable of subjecting it to the most scrupulous analysis.

In the first place, to understand thoroughly the singularity of my situation, you must completely throw aside all you have ever known of the easy amours of the poor lovelaces of your acquaintance. Those uncertain, ephemeral *liaisons* of lovers and mistresses with whom fancy is the only law, and which the slightest caprice can break, immoral and doubtful, which nothing guarantees, and where one elbows the rival of yesterday and the one of to-morrow. There is in all those love affairs something precarious and humiliating. In our customs there is no secret, no mystery; for all eyes may gaze upon the beauty of the most loving and the most beloved woman. It is like enjoying a certain property in common. In my harem, the charms of Zouhra, Nazli, and Kondjé-Gul, have never been looked upon except by my eyes; I know nothing of the trouble which the thought of a former rival always awakens. The future is no less sure than the present; their existence belongs to me; they are my slaves, I am their master.

I do not think I need recall to you that my interesting recital stopped at the first hour of the honeymoon. I returned to the chateau before my servants were up, went to bed and slept till midday. I breakfasted, and then waited till two o'clock before returning to El-Nouzha. Too great haste would have seemed to me vulgar. I wished to be both discreet and impassioned. Two o'clock seemed to me just the right hour.

I can not describe to you the state of mind in which I was. There are some troubles of the heart which defy analysis. The enchantment which held possession of me dulled my brain like the fumes of hasheesh, and I

scarcely recognized myself in the character of a hero of a
fairy tale; it cost me an effort to recall my identity, and
to assure myself that I was not dreaming. Then I
determined to go and see them. They were waiting for
me. They had doubtless already compared notes.
What reception should I meet with? My rôle of sultan
was so new to me that I was fearful of committing some
fault which should lower me in their eyes. I was going
blindly into this Mahomet's paradise, the laws of
which I knew nothing. Should I maintain the majestic
airs of a vizier, or abandon myself to the tender attitude
of a lover? In my perplexity, I was almost tempted to
appeal to Mohammed-Aziz to tell me the manners and
customs of a pacha of the shores of the Bosporus; but
perhaps that would spoil my happiness. To introduce a
hierarchy into my harem was a horrible idea to me; in
truth, the choice of a favorite would have been impossible. I loved them all four with an equal love, and I
could not even bear the thought of their being reduced
to three; my love in that case would have been incomplete.

Finally, as the hour had come without my having arrived
at any conclusion, I wisely decided to act according to
circumstances, and set out for my harem. I have
already told you, I think, that a little door of which I
alone had the key, connected my park with El-Nouzha;
then a sort of labyrinth led to Kasre; the path was long
and narrow and hidden in the undergrowth. As I
approached the garden, I saw Mohammed-Aziz, who
appeared to be watching for me, on the veranda. He ran
toward me and overwhelmed me with endless *salem aleks*.
I questioned him, and he answered me that I was expected.

At the same moment I heard cries of joy, and then the

sound of hasty footsteps and the rustle of silk, and
there soon appeared upon the veranda, disputing as to
who should arrive first, Hadidjé, Nazli, Kondjé-Gul, and
Zouhra. They all four threw themselves into my arms
with gay laughter, and held up their rosy lips to me,
each jealous for the first kiss. And all this with the
most child-like and ingenuous abandon! I was almost
going to say with so much innocence that I was utterly
overwhelmed with surprise; but, suddenly, at a word
from Mohammed, who was regarding us with a beaming
face, they appeared very much confused. He had,
doubtless, reproached them for a lack of decorum, for,
disengaging themselves gently, they drew back with
bended heads and their hands pressed to their foreheads.
You can easily imagine that I cut short these forms of
respect by clasping them again in my arms. Then there
were new peals of laughter, and jests with little victori-
ous airs at the expense of poor Mohammed. He raised
his hands to heaven with a bewildered air, as if bearing
witness that he had no share in this forgetfulness of all
Oriental etiquette. After this, I no longer paid any
attention to the difficulties I thought I should have to
encounter. I had imagined that my position would be a
delicate one; that I should have to witness a scene of
jealousy, rivalry, pique, coldness, perhaps even tears and
reproaches.

Five minutes afterward we went down into the
gardens. As they had only arrived the evening before,
they had not, till then, set foot outside the harem.
They were delighted with everything, and they chattered
away like young magpies. At each step they made
some new discovery, some mass of flowers, some shady
path, at the end of which bubbled a silvery fountain, its

waters running in little brooks across the park and into
the lake, and over which, here and there, were little
bridges painted in brilliant colors. They asked questions about everything. Kondjé-Gul was, of course, the
interpreter. They all listened, opening their great eyes,
and then ran off, gathering flowers, which they placed in
their hair, their bosoms, and about their necks. Every
once in awhile one of them would run back to me to
admire something she had found, or in quest of a kiss.

If you wish to know what a mortal thinks or feels in
such a position, I am forced to confess that it is not in
my power to inform you. I was captivated, enchanted,
and I gave myself up to enjoyment without a thought of
anything else. Besides, my dear fellow, for you to
understand it all, you need certain æsthetic notions
which you do not possess, artist though you are. You
would have to be acquainted with the exotic beauty
of the daughters of the Orient, with their child-
like ingenuousness and voluptuous nonchalance, with
their undulating movements, their supple grace, and
the fascination of their looks full of languor. It
would be necessary for you to have seen them in their
strange, picturesque costumes, the flowing silk trowsers
fastened at the ankles, the soft sash of cloth of gold
bound about the waist, the vests embroidered with pearls,
the waists of silk, transparent as gauze, the long robe
open in front, with the train caught up in the girdle to
aid them in walking; all this, and the exquisite colors
blending so charmingly together. It all formed such a
picture of grace and beauty that I give up all further
attempt at description.

After a time we reached a place where we were
obliged to cross a brook on stepping stones. I induced

Zouhra, who seemed to be the bravest, to cross it hand in hand with me. Hadidjé followed, but when it was Nazli's turn, she hung onto my neck in such terror at the great danger, that I took her in my arms and carried her over to the other side.

Kondjé-Gul, like a coquette, profited by the example. "Oh! carry me, too," she said.

As we reached the middle of the brook, one of her slippers fell into the water. You can imagine how we all laughed. Kondjé-Gul balanced herself on one foot while I fished out the tiny sandal. It then had to be dried in the sun in order not to soil her stocking of pale-green silk.

It was one of the prettiest places in all the park—a grassy carpet, shaded by a clump of sycamores. We sat down.

My friend, you have certainly seen a quantity of pictures called "A Dream of Happiness"—an enchanted garden; at the back the temple of Love; handsome young men and beautiful girls. Leave out of some such picture the details, which are a trifle too classical for Férouzat, and you can imagine me, stretched upon the grass, breathing in the fresh air and surrounded by my houris in the most adorable attitudes.

I threw my arm about Zouhra's neck, she placed her head on my shoulder. Hadidjé imitated her on the other side. I commenced to talk with Kondjé-Gul, the sole interpreter of my love. You probably guess that I was curious to know their thoughts.

"Then my country pleases you," I said to Kondjé-Gul, "and you are all glad you have come?"

"Oh, yes," she cried, "especially since we have seen you. Mohammed made us believe that you were old.

We feared a sad, severe life; so you can imagine how
glad we were yesterday when you came and he told us
that you were our master. At first, we did not dare to
believe him; but as he had allowed us to appear unveiled,
we saw that he could not be joking. And then, when I
heard you speak to him, I understood. Then I translated your words to the others, and told them you
thought us pretty."

"So," I said, "I may think that you love me, and they
also?"

She looked at me with astonishment, as if she did not
understand the sense of my question.

"Why, you are so good," she said, "so amiable, so
kind!"

The others listened attentively, without understanding
a word, their great eyes wandering from Kondjé-Gul to
me, and from me to Kondjé-Gul with an expression of
the greatest curiosity.

"And you," she continued, after a moment, "will you
really always love us, one just as much as the other, as
you do to-day?"

"Certainly," I answered with assurance, "that is the
custom in our harems. Is not that what you prefer?"

"Oh, yes!" she cried, "but we thought that you Franks
never loved more than one woman."

"That is said in Turkey to injure us, through jealousy, because ordinarily we only have one wife, to whom
we are bound to be faithful."

"But—when one has four, like you?" she asked.

"We are equally faithful to all four," said I, without
moving a muscle.

"Oh, what happiness!" she cried, clapping her hands
with joy.

And all at once, with the greatest volubility, she commenced to speak to the others, translating for them all
we had said. They were transported with delight.

Louis, don't go too far. I guess at your silly reflections in regard to this very simple situation, that you
permit yourself to stand up in judgment of, hampered
as you are by your ridiculous prejudices. Acknowledge
frankly, that in your feeble sphere of feelings, you are
quite ready to find my love eccentric. Under the falla-
cious pretext that it is not natural to be loved by four
women at once, like a miserable skeptic, you are capable
of wronging the sentiments which you can not understand. In the first place, you must know that they can
not conceive that there is the slightest irregularity in
their condition. According to the laws and customs of
their country, they believe themselves to be my wives, by
a bond quite as legitimate in their eyes as marriage is in
ours. They are my *cadines*, and this title gives them
duties and rights defined by the Koran itself.

Through condescension for your mediocre intelligence,
I will remark also, that under the blessed skies of Turkey, a woman never has the presumption and vanity to
desire a husband all to herself. Brought up for the
harem, the young girl has no other dream of ambition
than that of surpassing her rivals; but never, never has
she conceived the queer idea of being the sole object of
a lover's or a husband's affection. For Zouhra, Nazli,
Hadidjé, and Kondjé-Gul, the ideal existence is the one
I give them; they look upon it as the realization of all
their hopes. Their notions in regard to the destiny of
woman do not go beyond the happiness which they
enjoy, of pleasing and being loved. It is, therefore, useless to puzzle over your conventional ideas, and try to

draw from them a deduction in conformity with the regulations of the Orient.

The truth is that Hadidjé, Nazli, and Zouhra went
into transports of joy when Kondjé-Gul repeated to
them my promise to be faithful to all four.

My dear friend, there is much of the child in these
beings, who seem created only to give delight by their
beauty, like flowers are to exhale their perfume.   Clois-
tered in the life of the harem, their ideas do not go
beyond the harem's horizon.   Their minds and their
hearts have received no other cultivation than the recital
of marvelous legends and love-stories; they know nothing more.

Say, if you choose, that they are pretty little animals
who have no souls, but you will be wrong.   Once more,
the greater part of our ideas, so-called refined or civilized, upon love, virtue, propriety, modesty, are only
ideas which are in accordance with place, climate, or
habits.   My little animals show at times a daring abandon which resembles real innocence a thousand times
more than the prudish reserve of our well-brought-up
young ladies.

When the slipper was dry, Kondjé-Gul put it on her
little foot over the pale-green silk stocking, and we resumed our walk through the park.   We took a row on
the lake bordered with drooping willows.   The swans
and Chinese ducks followed in our wake.

Mohammed, with rare foresight, had made sure that I
should remain and dine at Kasre.   To-night the dinner
was served in the French style.   He was not present as
on the previous evening, I had no longer any need of
him, and he retired into the background.   I sat down to
table, therefore, with my houris, and the dinner, where

all was new to them, became a veritable fête. They
nibbled and tasted everything with little epicurean airs
indescribably graceful. I must say, however, that my
cook did not meet with unanimous favor till the dessert,
when they thoroughly enjoyed the preserves, cakes,
creams, and fruit. The champagne especially pleased
them, and it would have ended by mounting into their
little heads, if I had not been very careful. While they
laughed and chattered, I thought of the Oriental repast
of the previous evening, at which I had timidly seated
myself as a strange visitor. What wave of a fairy wand
had brought about this magical change?

I tell you it was enchantment! At dessert, Hadidjé
leaned toward me, with a mischievous air, and said laughingly some words in Turkish.

"*Sana yanarim!*" I answered, kissing her hand. I
had learned this phrase from Kondjé-Gul, and it means
"I love you," or rather, literally, "I burn for you."

You can imagine my success, and with what cries of
joy it was at first received. Then, naturally, there was a
scene of feigned jealousy by the others. "*Kianet! ah!
kianet!*" they repeated, laughing and threatening me.
This word means "ingrate."

When it was evening, to calm their overflowing spirits,
I led them into the park. It was a magnificent moonlight
night, and the trees threw long shadows upon the sward.
When we passed through the dark places, they clung
timidly to me.

You do not expect me to tell you, I suppose, how the
day ended. *Affaires du harem, mon cher, affaires du harem.*

As for other news from here, I need not tell you that
no one in the place suspects the secrets of El-Nouzha.
My life, to all outward appearance, is in strict conformity

with my position. I visit my uncle's old friends, Féraudet
the notary, and the good old *curé* who calls me the prov-
idence of the place. Once a week I dine with Dr.
Morand, who has a son, George Morand, an officer of
the Spahis, just now on leave at Férouzat, and an orphan
niece, a young girl of nineteen, very sweet and sympathetic.
She is betrothed to her cousin, the captain; he is a regular type of the African soldier, but a good fellow in
every acceptation of the word; one of those frank
natures made for devotion, like the Newfoundland dog, at
once formidable and patient; he is my friend. We were
playmates when we were children and he would not allow
anyone to speak ill of me in his presence. He is very
much astonished at my hermit life and that I do not join
him in any gaiety or pleasure.

CHAPTER VI.

In relating to you minutely the events of the first day
of my honeymoon, my dear Louis, I have given you an
account of the way almost every day has been passed
since my last letter. "Happy people have no history,"
said a wise man; happiness has nothing to tell. In the
first place, you must understand that I write you now
entirely recovered from the natural bewilderment conse-
quent upon my strange adventure. Three months have
rolled by; I enjoy my happiness like a fastidious vizier
and no longer as a simple Provençal troubadour, astray
in the caliph's harem. In fact I have recovered my
powers of cool analysis.

As you may well believe, on the second day, I set
myself to work studying Turkish, an easy task after my

Sanscrit studies. On the other hand, love aiding them, my houris have learned French with that marvelous gift, that instinct for language which the natives of Asia possess, and you will not be astonished to hear that I can enjoy to-day conversing with them all; this fortunate result will permit me to study their different characters.

To allow you completely to understand my story, I will give you in the present letter the most circumstantial details upon the following subjects:

1. The organization, laws, and internal regulations of my harem.

2. A description of my odalisques and their respective characters.

3. An elaborate essay upon the advantages of polygamy and its application to the moral regeneration of man.

I will confess in the first place, without any presumption, that the ingenious system established for the management of my harem is entirely to the honor of my uncle Barbassou, who was always, like a man of the world, particularly careful to observe all the laws of what the English call respectability. Throughout all the place, and even in the eyes of my servants, Mohammed-Aziz passes for an exile, a high political personage to whom my uncle offered hospitality. Barbassou-Pacha always addressed him respectfully as " Your Excellency," and no domestic of the chateau speaks of him in any other terms. He has had the misfortune to lose one of his daughters, for, it seems, he once had five. Are they young or are they old? No one knows. Within Kasre, the servants are all Greek women who never go out of the grounds, and do not know a word of French. The gardeners are obliged to quit the gardens before nine o'clock in the morning. All this, as you see, is very correct. Mohammed's story is most plausible; his air of majestic sadness and his solitary life are quite in accordance with the fallen grandeur of a minister in disgrace. He is writing, it is said, his memoirs and it is even known that I am often with him to aid him in that task.

Every day, about three o'clock, after having devoted the morning to my business or my " Essays upon Psychology," I go to El-Nouzha, and I generally remain there the rest of the day. I am giving my houris swimming lessons. Barbassou-Pacha has created a marvel in the way of a bath-house. In the middle of an island in the lake (which is copied from the one in the superb gardens of Lse-ma-kouang, the famous Chinese poet,) imagine a great marble basin, surrounded by a circular wall, a sort of atrium, open to the skies. A piazza runs all about it, protected by awnings and spread with Persian rugs. In the interior, the walls are decorated with frescoes, copied from Herculaneum and Pompeii. About the white columns cluster roses and myrtle. The enchanting place is furnished with leather divans, hammocks, carpets, and cushions. We often have breakfast here on hot days, and I am now reclining here writing to you, surrounded by my harem, which naturally affords me an excellent opportunity to give you a description of my almehs.

Kondjé-Gul, the nonchalant beauty who is swinging below there in her hammock, is a Circassian by race. Her name signifies, in Turkish, a species of rose with which we are not acquainted; she was taken to Constantinople, when quite young, by her mother, who was attached to the sultan's service; she is now eighteen Imagine the Circassian type in all its glory. Tall, with the

figure of a young goddess, and with an air of natural
indolence which seems to indicate a consciousness of her
queen-like beauty. Her small shapely head is covered
with a wealth of chestnut hair falling below her waist.
Her features are wonderfully pure and delicate. Her
eyes are large, brown, and languishing; shaded with
thick, black eyelashes; her lips a trifle full and pouting,
seeming always to invite a kiss; in fact, her beauty is
Grecian, with a sort of odd grace peculiar to that Tcher-
kesse race, still a little savage, which I can no more
adequately describe than I could explain to you the perfume of the lily. Loving and tender, she is, however,
the jealous element in my household—but hush! the
others don't know it. She is assuredly the strangest
and the most perfect of my little savages.

Hadidjé is a Jewess from Samos, a Jewess of a singularly rare type among the descendants of Israel. She is
a blonde, a golden blonde, of which the paintings of
Paul Veronese can give you some idea. Imagine Byron's
"Bride of Abydos," or the heroine of the "Giaour;" place
her in the atmosphere of the harem, which orientalizes
her grace, and gives that peculiar Eastern allurement,
and you ——

My friend, something incredible, surprising, unheard-
of, amazing, supernatural, has happened! Do not
attempt to guess what it is, you would never discover it!
Never! Never! It surpasses the most wonderful, the
most miraculous occurrence that a human brain could
imagine.

Yesterday I was interrupted in my letter by Hadidjé
at the very moment I was drawing her portrait. The
day passed without my finding the leisure to finish it.
This morning I was breakfasting at the chateau, quite

alone in my study, where I ordinarily have breakfast
served in order not to interrupt my work. I was reading
the last number of a scientific review, when my ear was
struck by the sound of carriage wheels on the gravel
outside. As I have very few visitors, and as my friend
George, the Spahi, always comes on foot, I thought it
was my notary come to consult me on business, which he
has reproached me for the last two weeks with neglecting.
The carriage stopped before the door. I heard the
servants cross the hall. Suddenly there was a cry, then
a confused murmur of voices full of alarm, and then the
sound of hurried footsteps fleeing in affright.

I listened in astonishment, when suddenly a stentorian
voice pronounced these words:

"What is the matter with those idiots? Do you mean
to leave me here all day with my luggage?"

Louis, imagine my stupefaction. I thought I recognized the voice of my deceased uncle.

"François!" I heard again like a trumpet. "You
shall suffer for this, you animal!"

I rose, ran to the window, and saw distinctly my uncle
Barbassou himself.

"Ah! are you there, my boy?" he said.

I ran down to the door and seized both his hands,
You can imagine my emotion and surprise. The servants regarded us from a distance, too frightened to
approach.

"Well?" said my uncle. "What is the matter with
them? Have I horns on my head?"

"I will explain it to you presently," said I. "Come
in and I will have your luggage attended to."

"All right," he answered, "and give me some breakfast. I am as hungry as a wolf."

This was said with the calmness of a man who is never
astonished at anything, and with a strong Marseillaise
accent.   My uncle speaks seven languages. In Paris,
as you know, he speaks with the purity of a Parisian, but
when he sets foot in Provence, he speaks with an accent.

He entered with a brisk step, and I followed him.
When he reached the study and saw the table set, he sat
down as quietly as if he had just returned from a walk in
the park, poured out two great glasses of wine and swal-
lowed them one after the other with a deep sigh of satisfaction.   Then he commenced to attack the various
dishes with such a tremendous appetite that it was
utterly impossible to take him for a spectre. I did not
interrupt him, but gazed at him with amazement until he
had finished.   Then I said to him:

" Where do you come from, uncle?"

"I come from Japan, you know that," he answered, as
if speaking of some neighboring town.   " Only I have
not come directly from there, and I had no time to write
to you."

"And what have you been doing for the last five
months?"

"Oh!   I went to Abyssinia to see the king, who owed
me 200,000 francs.   He did not pay me, though, the
rascal!   But you look very queer.   And François opens
his eyes at me as though I were going to swallow him.
Do I look so ferocious?   By the way, you have changed
my liveries.   The servants look like priests.   Have you
made them take holy orders?"

" But, uncle, for five months we have worn mourning
for you."

" Worn mourning for me?   You are joking."

" For five months we have believed you to be dead.

We received all the documents attesting your de-
cease."

"And these documents said I was buried, perhaps?"
asked my uncle, without betraying the slightest emotion.

"Certainly," I answered, "we have, also, the certificate
of your burial."

At this my uncle could no longer contain himself, but
shook with one of those paroxysms of silent laughter
peculiar to him.

"In that case, you were my heir," he said, when his
merriment permitted him to speak.

"Yes, uncle, and I am already in possession of your
property."

This answer started him off again, and his laughter
was so infectious that both François and I joined in it.
But suddenly my uncle grew grave, as if struck by some
reflection, and seizing my hand he said: •

"Ah! this reappearance of mine must be a great blow
to you, my boy."

This was said with so much frankness and in such a
pitying tone, that I assure you I was deeply moved, and
the tears came into my eyes.

"There, there," he said, tapping me on the shoulder,
"don't be a goose. I am here; you need not mourn me
any longer."

After the table was cleared and we were alone, I
said to him, "Now, uncle, when you have explained
to me how this mistake came about, we must make haste
and take the necessary steps to prove your resuscitation."

"Prove my resuscitation!" he cried. "What for?"

"To re-establish your civil status and your rights as a
living man."

4

"Anyone who sees me will know that I am not in the other world," he replied, tranquilly.

" But since you are considered as dead, you will not be able to do anything, to sign anything, or to make any contract."

" There, there, never mind! Barbassou-Pacha is not going to bother himself about such a little thing as that."

" But your property and estates which I have inherited?"

" Have you paid the administration fees?" he asked, seriously.

" Certainly, uncle."

" Well, then; do you want to pay double to enrich the Government? You would have to pay them all over again when I really die."

" What do you mean to do then?"

" Oh! you keep the stuff. It is your turn now," he added. " I have held the purse for forty years; it is now your turn, my boy. You administer and take care of the property now, and you must pay the expenses for everything."

" You must not think of that, uncle!" I cried. " Even supposing I should continue to manage your fortune ——"

" Pardon me," he interrupted, "*your* fortune! You paid the fees."

" *Our* fortune, then, if you like," I continued, laughing. " It is none the less true, I repeat, that you can not remain in a state of civil death."

" Bah! Bah! Political ideas! In the first place, explain to me how I died, for that puzzles me."

I told him what you already know of this strange history; the letter of the notary telling me the cruel news brought by his mate, Lieutenant Rabassu, confirmed by the most authentic certificates, and accompanied by a pocket-book containing all his papers, letters, property in his name, contracts signed by him; in fact, incontestable proofs that the story was true.

"My papers!" he cried.   "They were not lost, then?"

"I have them all," I answered.

"I understand, now.   It is the fault of that fool of a Lefébure."

"Who is Lefébure?" I asked.

"I will tell you, presently; all is explained and clear, now.   But, by the way, with the news of my death did not Rabassu bring some camels?"

"Not a camel, uncle."

"That is strange.   But sit down, and I will tell you all about it."

I sat down and my uncle told me the following story. I will transcribe it for you faithfully, my dear Louis, but what I can not render is the inimitable calmness with which he related it, as if he were speaking of some village festival.

"In returning from Japan," he said, "I touched at Java.   Naturally, I went on shore.   On the wharf I met Lefébure, an old sailor-friend of mine; he had left the sea and married a mulattress who sold tobacco.   I said to him, 'Holloa! how are you?' He shook my hand and answered, 'Bored to death.' 'Bored!' I replied. 'Well, come and pass a few days with me at Toulon; my ship is here in port and I will send you back next month on the "Belle-Virginie."' My proposal delighted him, but he answered, 'It is impossible.' 'Impossible! Why?' 'Because I have a wife who wouldn't like it.' 'We will see

about that.' We went to the shop; his wife made a
scene, screamed, and cried. Finally, when she became
somewhat quieted, I said: 'I shall weigh anchor this
evening at six. I will wait for you till five minutes past.'
I then went about my business. At six o'clock I weighed
anchor. At five minutes past I was about to depart
when I saw a boat approaching. It was Lefébure. He
came alongside, boarded us, and we set sail. Fifteen
days afterward we touched for a few hours at Ceylon.
The twenty-sixth day, sailing into the harbor of Aden,
we passed an English man-of-war carrying an admiral's
flag, which we saluted. I learned on land that she had
brought an embassy charged with a message to the King
of Abyssinia. And there I met Captain Picklock, one of
my old friends whom I knew at Calcutta, where he commanded the Sepoys. He told me that he was the head
of the embassy. I said to Lefébure: 'Look here, the
king owes me something; shall we make a call on him?'
'All right,' answered Lefébure. I bought four horses
and six camels which I loaded with provisions, and we
departed with the embassy. We had quite a pleasant
time on the journey. I already knew the country, but
about half way, at Adona, where we halted for half a
day, Lefébure got acquainted with an Arab woman. He
wanted to remain a day or two, and said to me: 'Go with
the captain, and I will rejoin you to-morrow with the
camels and the baggage. I departed. The next day
no Lefébure. That annoyed me because he had kept
the camels. However, I continued my journey thinking
I should meet him on my return. In short, I reached
the king's capital only to learn that he had just been
dethroned. I intended to appeal to the English to help
me arrange my little affair, when I perceived that I had

left my pocket-book and papers with Lefébure, who had the
baggage. Fortunately, I had some gold in my belt. Then
I took advantage of the opportunity to take a little trip
into Nubia, where I had some acquaintances. I charged
Captain Picklock to tell Lefébure to come and join me
at Lennaar with the camels. Then I departed. At the
end of ten days I reached Lennaar and found the King
of Nubia. He was not very secure in his position, but
he was very friendly, and I bought some ivory and ostrich
feathers from him.

"Three weeks passed—no Lefébure! Then I naturally took advantage of the occasion to push on a little
into Darfour. But on the ninth day, as I reached the
neighborhood of El Obéïd, in Kordofan, I encountered a
tribe of Changalla robbers. They surrounded me. I
tried to defend myself, when a tall, heavy fellow seized
me round the neck. I was almost strangled, but I hit
him a blow in the stomach which laid him low. The
others, however, attacked me on all sides and I was taken
prisoner. It seems my blow had killed the negro. That
did not better my situation. They dragged me
into a hut and bound me, after having stolen all my
gold.

"I was well guarded. At the end of eight days I said
to myself, 'Barbassou, your ship is in port at Aden; you
have business to attend to; you must negotiate for a
ransom and resign yourself to a sacrifice.' I sent for the
chief, and proposed to him for my ransom fifty bottles
of rum, ten muskets, and two complete English uniforms.
This offer tempted him, but as I asked to be conducted
first to the King of Nubia, he answered that once there I
would tell him to go to the devil. Finally, at the end of
four months, after numerous discussions, we agreed that

I should be taken to Lennaar, where I promised on my word of honor to give guarantees for the ransom. I departed, still bound, and guarded by ten men. In fifteen days we entered the city. I sought Lefébure, but no Lefébure could I find. I went to see the king. He had gone away on an eight days' hunting expedition. However, I found the governor and told him my story. He answered that the treasury was closed. I told the men who accompanied me to return and that I would send them the ransom from Aden. This did not content them, but the governor interfered and gave me an escort to Gondar. The English had left, so I set out for Aden. When I arrived at Adona, where I had left my friend, I asked for Lefébure. No Lefébure to be found. Finally, I chanced to meet his Arab woman. I questioned her. She told me that the very day I left him he received a sun-stroke from which he died the same day. I sought for my baggage and my camels. No baggage; no camels. They had all been sent to the governor of Aden. I reached Aden and the governor told me that all my effects had been sent on board ship with the papers found on my friend and a certificate of his death, which my mate took charge of to send to his family. I made no further inquiries. I wrote at once a short letter of condolence to Lefébure's widow. I sent the Changallas the ransom agreed on, and at the same time a letter of complaint to the King of Nubia. My ship had sailed four months before. The next day I took the Suez steamer. I arrived at Marseilles last night; and here I am!"

"Indeed," I said to my uncle, after he had finished, "all is explained. The certificate of death was among the papers found on your friend, Lefébure, and as those papers were yours ——"

"They made a mistake, and that imbecile of a Rabassu set out to bear the news of my death to the notary."

"It is all clear, now," I added.

"But what troubles me the most," he said, "is to know what has become of my camels."

CHAPTER VII.

This unexpected resurrection of my uncle, my dear Louis, occupied all my thoughts to the exclusion of every-thing else. I cared only to see him, to hear him, and I so completely forgot everything except what pertained to him that I never once thought all day of putting my foot out of the chateau. I followed him from room to room, I gazed at him with all my eyes. I wanted to con-vince myself that he was indeed in the flesh. As for him, he quickly recovered from his slight astonishment at the news of his death, and unpacked, himself, his trunks, full of all sorts of curiosities from Nubia, whistling softly to himself wild African airs.

In the evening, while we were sipping our coffee, he said to me, stretching his long legs on the divan, like a man enjoying his ease:

"Well, we are very well off in this place. If you like, we will stay some weeks here."

"As many weeks as you choose, uncle," I answered, "and even months."

"Good! But aren't you bored here? For certainly there is no distraction——"

"Oh!" I cried, suddenly recalling my harem. "I for-got to speak to you of something."

"What! There is a distraction then?"

"Yes, indeed, uncle."

"Is she pretty?"

"There are four of them."

At these words my uncle showed no more emotion than if I had told him that I practiced the cornet to while away my time; only he stretched out his arm, seized my hand, shook it, and said:

"I congratulate you, and I ask pardon for my indiscreet question."

"But, uncle, this is quite a story!" I added, not without some embarrassment. "And it is your death which was the cause of it all."

"Indeed! How so? Tell me about it."

"You know your Turkish pavilion, Kasre-el-Nouzha?"

"I know it. Well?"

"Well, four months ago, Mohammed-Aziz arrived."

"Ah!" he said. "Mohammed?"

"And you had charged him—with a commission," I continued.

"That is true," he exclaimed. "I had forgotten that."

"Then—uncle——"

"He had fulfilled his commission?"

"Yes," I answered. "And as you were dead, and as Mohammed's commission formed part of your property, I thought that I ought——"

"By Jove!" said my uncle. "You're a fine heir!"

"Why," I said, hesitating a little, "remember, I could not suppose——"

"Well," he said, "say no more about it, and once more pardon me. Now that I know it, there is nothing more to be said. Affairs of the harem are never discussed among Turks. Only," he added, "I advise you to keep Mohammed; he is a good man for his place. And, for more security, as I can not go there, tell him to come and see me."

"Shall I send for him at once?"

"No, no; to-morrow; we have time enough. Now, give me a little music, will you? Play me something from Verdi."

And he commenced to sing in his deep bass voice something intended for "*Parigi, ó cara.*"

We passed a delightful evening: conversation, music, and cards. He won three francs from me at piquet, to his great delight. About midnight, I showed him to his chamber. As he was preparing for bed, "There," he cried, "I have some valuables I had forgotten." And taking a knife, he cut the lining of his coat and drew out some papers.

"Here!" he said, handing them to me. "Here are 700,000 francs in drafts on London and Paris. You can get them cashed."

"Very well, uncle," I answered. "And what do you wish me to do with the money."

"Oh! that's your own concern, my lad! Remember, now that you have inherited my property, I don't want to have anything to do with those matters."

"At least, advise me."

"But then I should have the trouble of it still. No, keep it. It will serve you to furnish me with pocket money."

He then retired. I wished him good-night, and was about to leave the room when he called me back.

"Look here, André, write to the notary to come here to-morrow."

"Ah!" I exclaimed, "you have come to that conclusion at last, have you?"

"I have come to no conclusion at all," he cried in the most decided tone. "I wish to know what has be-come of my camels. You see, I intended to present them to the Zoölogical Society. They must be found! Good-night."

CHAPTER VIII.

Surely, my dear Louis, I need not call your attention to the strange character of the events which have taken place during the last four months. I do not think any human being ever experienced such before. The nota-ry's sad letter, my installation at Férouzat, my uncle's will, the arrival of the harem from Turkey, the taking possession of my inheritance, and the whole crowned by the return of the defunct. Certainly, you must confess that those are incidents which are not encountered every day. Only, if you wish to know my thoughts, I must say that all this seems to me, now, only cause and effect in their simplest form. I do not even see how it could be otherwise with my uncle's nephew, for it would show a woeful ignorance of the first principles of logic to be astonished at these particular experiences, when Barbas-sou-Pacha is once introduced as *first cause.* My uncle ex-ercises such a powerful influence over my destiny, that it would be entirely paradoxical, in my opinion, to suppose that things could happen to me as to anyone else. Like those foolish planets which deviate at times from their course, I circle about that wonderful star called Barbas-sou-Pacha, and he draws me into his extravagant orbit. In spite of a vain appearance of romantic complications, in the very simple facts I have related to you, I defy you to find the slightest grain of improbability; it has all come about by the most natural means. Cease being astonished, then, if you do not wish to fall to the lowest rank in my esteem.

Recalling to your memory, therefore, that I am my uncle's nephew, I resume my tale. You know that my late uncle has come to life, but that he wishes to keep his advantages as a dead man by forcing me to remain in possession of his property. You remember that I bade him good-night, leaving him to dream of his camels. Nothing could be less complicated than that, and all strictly in accordance with Claude Anatole Barbassou's character. But the day of his return was marked by another incident of some importance.

I left my uncle and went to the library to write at once to the notary, when François told me that a woman from Kasre had been waiting for me for an hour. One of the Greek servants came sometimes to the chateau, either with messages or to ask for orders. I saw at once that, as they had not seen me all day, my houris had become anxious and had sent to find out what was the matter. I went to my chamber, where François told me she was. As I entered, I perceived her, standing motionless near the window, wrapped in a dark-colored *feridjié;* but I had scarcely closed the door behind me, when I heard a cry and a sob. The *feridjié* fell to the ground, and I recognized Kondjé-Gul, who threw herself on my neck, and seized me with the most violent despair.

"What, is it you?" I said. "You have come here?"

Breathless and suffocated by her tears, she could not answer me. I guessed at rather than heard these words: "I have run away and come to die with you."

"But you are mad, mad, mad!" I cried. "Why do you speak of dying? What has happened?"

"Oh! we know all!" she replied. "Barbassou-Pacha has returned! He will kill you, and us too, and Mohammed too!"

And she clung to me with all her strength, as if already threatened with death.

"But my child," I said, "this is pure folly. Who has told you all this?"

"Mohammed. He learned of the pacha's return and he has hidden himself."

"Why, my uncle is very good; he is very fond of me. He does not even dream of seeing you; his return will make no difference in your life."

As she saw me so calm, she gradually became reassured; but she was too much imbued with Turkish ideas to admit, at once, such a derogation from Turkish customs.

"Then," she said, drying her tears, "he will only kill Mohammed."

"Not even Mohammed!" I exclaimed, laughing. "Mohammed is a poltroon who shall be well scolded to-morrow, to prevent him from telling you any more such ridiculous stories."

"Is that really true, and he will only be beaten?"

I saw if I denied the beating too, she would suspect that I was trying to deceive her, and her fears would be awakened again even more vividly, so I simply contented myself with promising to intercede with Barbassou-Pacha. Once convinced that Mohammed would suffer nothing worse than a beating, she thought no more about it, and with one of those quick transitions which characterize these little savage beings, she commenced to laugh and talk, examining all the articles in my room and touching everything with the greatest curiosity.

"Come, now, you must return," I said to her, having no desire that her escapade should be discovered.

"Oh no! Oh no!" she cried, with the gaiety of a child. "This is your house; let me see it."

"But, Zouhra, Nazli, and Hadidjé must be reassured."

"Oh! they are asleep. I want to stay here a little while, all alone with you. Besides," she added, with a little frightened look, "suppose Barbassou-Pacha has deceived you and is coming to-night to kill you?"

"Once more, I tell you, that is perfectly senseless."

"Well, then, why do you send me away so quickly?"

"Because it was not right for you to leave the harem. Come!"

"Oh! wait a little while, just a little while!" she said, entreatingly.

How could I resist, my dear Louis?

I sat down, watching her running about and fumbling over everything. I must tell you that, under her *feridjé* which she had cast aside on my entrance, she wore a sort of floating robe of pale-blue cashmere, embroidered with brilliant designs in silk and gold. From the long flowing sleeves appeared her beautiful white arms. She produced a most charming and picturesque effect in my apartment, so prosaic in its comfort, but which, however, seemed to her marvelous. She touched everything, wanted to see everything, and her questions never ceased. At the end of half an hour, thinking her curiosity satisfied, as she was beginning to turn over the books on the table, I said:

"Come Kondjé-Gul, you must go."

I wrapped her in her *feridjé* and led her back to the harem. A pale light shone from the windows of the

salon. Hadidjé, Nazli, and Zouhra were still there. To
depict the terror which seized them when I entered,
would be impossible. Hearing some one approaching
at night, they did not doubt that their last moment had
come. At the sound of the door opening, they uttered
a scream and the three poor little things took refuge in
a corner.

When they perceived me with Kondjé-Gul, they were
astounded, but I soon calmed their fears.

Mohammed was nowhere to be found. To tell the
truth, I did not try very hard to discover his hiding-
place; I was not sorry to have him pass an uncomfort-
able night to punish him for his folly in alarming my poor
houris.

CHAPTER IX.

I beg your pardon, my dear Louis, for having left
you for a month without a letter, and for which you
somewhat bitterly reproach me. I hope you do not
think that my friendship is any the less, but the fact
is, I have had nothing to tell you. My days are one
very like the other, taken up with my harem and my
uncle. I have enjoyed the quiet of the fields and the
woods, which give me that peace which I never find in
the busy, feverish atmosphere of the city.

Don't think, however, that we live like hermits, my
uncle and I, disdaining all worldly distractions; the
captain is not a man to live a lazy life; he is as much on
horseback as on foot. In the day we make excursions,
go hunting, and he visits my estates; I assure you he
makes a capital steward. In the evening, we have com-

pany at the chateau; the *curé*, the Morands, father and
son, and twice a week the notary. We play whist at two
sous the corner, and piquet, only the latter game very
rarely, because my uncle cheats. About eleven o'clock
the carriages are brought round and our guests depart.
I accompany my uncle to his room, we talk of our business, of my fiancée, for of course my marriage with his
god-daughter is arranged, and the idea has never come
to either of us to disagree on that point. We have, beside, a very serious occupation, which consists in bringing
to light the many marvels stored in the attics of the
chateau.

"By the way, André," my uncle said to me one day
in the reproachful tone of a faithful factotum, "You have
a quantity of beautiful things up-stairs that you are very
foolish to leave there. If I were you, I should bring
them down."

"We will do so, uncle," I answered.

So we set to work, and you have no idea of all that
we have found; costly cloths, objects of art, rare pieces
of furniture, arms and weapons of all countries. You
shall see what a collection it is, if you ever come here;
indeed, for an artist like you, it would be well worth your
while to drop in on us for that purpose alone.

We also make calls at the two chateaux of the locality,
owned by the Montaubecs and the Camboulions; but
only as often as politeness demands, the feminine element we meet there being classed by my uncle in the
very lowest ranks of inferior zoology.

Once a week we dine with Dr. Morand, a man of great
talents, who only requires a larger sphere of action, and
the only man who could have any influence over Captain
Barbassou, if Captain Barbassou's character was such as

could be influenced by any one. Dr. Morand's house
presents a perfect picture of domestic happiness, filled as
it is with a raft of children. I have already spoken to
you of his son, the Spahi, and of his niece, Genevieve.

Genevieve is nineteen, and much older than any of
her brothers and sisters, who are the offspring of her
mother's second marriage. The doctor, who is rich for
this part of the country, received them all at his sister's
death. Nothing could be more charming than this household, where one breathes in the atmosphere the perfume
of peaceful happiness and purity. You should see Genevieve surrounded by her little rosy brothers and sisters,
all clean and healthy, at once mischievous and obedient,
and whom she rules with a youthful wisdom, which is
not always exempt itself from a suspicion of roguery. Is
she pretty? I confess that I don't know; she has such a
charm of manner that you never think whether she is
pretty or not. She has certainly beautiful eyes, full of
expression. George Morand, her betrothed, adores her,
and submits to her slightest wish. They were made for
one another, and will certainly be happy. She will
correct the soldier's rather too impetuous nature.

My uncle professes to detest children; I need not add
that when the captain arrives, the whole brood rush to
him and clamber all over him. He plays horse with
them, and builds them houses of blocks. And the other
day you should have seen him, growling all the time,
sewing a button on Toto's jacket, which he had pulled
off in play, for fear Genevieve would scold.

I am very cordially treated by all the household, and
you can imagine what discussions the doctor and I have.
He was formerly a professor in the Montpellier College,
and his physiological studies have led him to downright

materialism. As he has read and re-read my spiritual-
istic articles, he strives to convince me. On the other
hand, my uncle, a Mohammedan, wishes to convert him.
So you can see what lively times we sometimes have.

At El-Nouzha, the same life goes on. My harem is
now the most peaceful domestic retreat, and except that I
have four wives instead of one, everything proceeds as
quietly as in the simplest and most ordinary household.
In the evening, we talk, seated about the table in the
salon, we have music and we dance, sometimes varied
by the education of my sultanas. I mingle the Oriental
magnificence of a vizier with the tender sentimentality
of a Galaor; in short, it is a Mahomet's paradise, were it
not that, since my uncle's return, a few clouds have
obscured the radiance of my honeymoon. I have had
quarrels with Hadidjé and Nazli, who insisted on going
to the chateau, like Kondjé-Gul; for you see that, after
their excitement had cooled down, that goose of a
Kondjé-Gul, to arouse their jealousy doubtless, and to
give herself the airs of a favorite, did not fail to tell
them the marvels of the place which was forbidden to
them. Naturally, I squarely refused to consent to any
such expedition, so contrary to all the traditions of the
harem. Then, of course, there was a scene of tears and
anger, which I appeased, and which turned into the
tender reproaches of neglected wives. In fact, what
shall I say to you? I humor them as far as I can, like
all husbands, but I feel vaguely that the air is full of
electricity.

I open my letter to add a few lines.

My friend, you must not be astonished. I have a
piece of news relative to Barbassou-Pacha.

The day before yesterday, when, as usual, I was talking

in the evening by my uncle's bedside, I saw that he yawned in an unusual manner. I had already noticed this symptom, and I concluded that his innate instincts for an adventurous life had awakened in him, and that he was beginning to find his life in Provence too narrow and restricted. Certainly, something was lacking. And I was seeking to discover what new amusement I could invent to satisfy his devouring activity, when, as I was leaving him, he said:

"By the way, André, I have written to your aunt announcing my return. She will probably arrive here the end of the week."

"Ah!" I answered. "Well, that is good, uncle, and I shall be delighted to see you a family man."

"Yes, she will ornament the house," he answered.

"Good-night, my boy."

"Good-night, uncle."

Although nothing could be more natural than my uncle's desire to have his wife with him, you can understand that I was somewhat bewildered by it. Which of my aunts was coming? My uncle had spoken in such a natural way that I never dreamed of asking him any question which could be in the slightest degree indiscreet. I therefore tried to conjecture, taking into consideration the state of his mind, to which of his wives he had given the preference.

I threw aside at once my aunt Cora of the Isle of Bourbon. It was hardly probable that the pacha wished to add anything to his ontological work on races of color. My aunt Christine, of Postero, whose adventure with Jean Bonaffé merited disgrace, also excluded, there only remained my aunt Lia Ben Lévy, my aunt Gretchen van Cloth, and my aunt Eudoxie de Cornalis, which

restricted the question considerably; but I acknowledge
that it was in vain I set to work all my faculties of
induction, considering the captain's age, his present tastes
and his plans. I only succeeded in losing myself in a
labyrinth of doubts and guesses. The best thing I could
do was to wait. So waiting I am.

CHAPTER X.

I did not have to wait a long time, however, for two
days later, before I had left my room, I saw a carriage
approaching. A lady, who appeared to me very beautiful, and very elegant, was seated alone in it. Upon the
box, beside the coachman, was a maid; behind, two
stylish footmen in livery. The carriage stopped before the
door. At the sound of the wheels upon the gravel, my
uncle's window opened.

"Ah! good-morning, my dear," he cried.

"Good-morning, captain," answered the lady; "you
see that you are not forgotten, ingrate!"

"Thank you; I also am not forgetful."

"That is all very well," responded the lady, "but you
don't come down to help me out; you are not gallant."

"Wait," said my uncle, "I will come at once."

I confess that I was a little puzzled at sight of the
traveler, whose grand air recalled none of my aunts.
Had Barbassou-Pacha contracted a new marriage since
making his will? I discreetly determined not to be present at their meeting, but as my uncle passed my door, he
called out:

"André, are you coming?"

I followed him. When we reached the door, the lady was coming up the steps.

"Too late, captain! I could not remain there, shut up in that carriage."

They shook hands, however, with the greatest cordiality; as I was watching them, my uncle said coolly:

"This is your aunt Eudoxie, André."

Thus informed, I stepped forward and greeted my aunt Eudoxie.

"What, is it André?" she cried: "Oh, pardon my familiarity, monsieur; but I was thinking of the pretty boy I once knew."

"Please continue to call me André, I beg of you, madame," I answered.

"Oh, no; not if you call me madame."

"Aunt, then; I shall be delighted to return to the familiar terms of the past, if you will allow me."

"Well, nephew," she added, "give orders to have my people taken care of, and let us go in."

All this was said with the easy grace of a woman accustomed to the best society, which for a moment almost made me feel awkward. My childish remembrance was of a young, amiable, and charming woman, but I had not expected to see the elegant person before me. I surely should never have recognized her, although time had scarcely altered her beauty.

Imagine a woman about thirty-five, although she must be at least forty-two, of rather pronounced *embonpoint*, perhaps, which, however, detracts nothing from her grace, for she is very tall, and even adds something to her patrician air. Her manners are exceedingly refined and high-bred, but at the same time very simple. Her

voice is like velvet, with the slight singing accent peculiar to the Russians.

My uncle offered her his arm, and led her to the *salon*.

"Now," she said, removing her hat, "you must explain to me at once how it was that you were reported
to have departed this life. For six months I have believed myself to be a widow."

"You have only to look at me to be convinced of the
contrary," answered my uncle.

"I am only too glad to find the report false!" she exclaimed, laughing, and taking his hand. "It was only
another of your eccentricities, I suppose."

"Not at all, my dear; André, here, will tell you that I
was really supposed to be dead, and that he wore mourning for me. He even inherited my property."

"It is an ill wind that blows nobody good," she replied. "But how did the mistake happen? I don't
understand."

"I was in Abyssinia——"

"Near here?" she interrupted.

"Yes," replied my uncle. "A friend who was with
me remained behind, while I went on further. He died;
and as he had with him my luggage and papers, he was
mistaken for me. I did not know until my return here
five months later that I was supposed to be dead. You
see how simple it all was?"

"In fact," said my aunt, "such a thing might have
happened to anyone. That will teach you to always take
me with you in your journeys. Was it on account of
this visit to Abyssinia that I have not seen you for two
years? Don't go, nephew," she added in a pleasant
tone, "a domestic scene will be instructive to you.
Well, answer, captain."

"Two years?" replied my uncle, "is it really two years?"

"Consult your ship's papers, if they are not buried with your friend."

"Pardon me, dear Eudoxie, but I have had so much business to attend to."

"Yes," replied my aunt, "your great enterprises are known, and I have heard some fine things about you. Do you know what Lord Cliefden said to me at St. Petersburg, complimenting me on the becomingness of my mourning? He told me that you had committed bigamy."

"How probable that is!" exclaimed my uncle, with perfect self-control.

"He declared that he saw you at Madras with a young and pretty Spaniard, wretch that you are, who passed everywhere under the name of Señora Barbassou. You had better not have eloped with me, if you were going to treat me like that!"

"Lord Cliefden was jesting, my dear, and a very sorry jest it was. I hope you did not believe him?"

"I don't know; you are so very eccentric," she answered, laughing.

"And what have you been doing?" asked my uncle, whose coolness had not for an instant deserted him; "where have you been?"

"Oh, if I should go back to the day of your departure, I could not remember," answered my aunt. "A year ago at this time I was on my estates in the Crimea, where I was bored to death for five months; then I passed the winter in St. Petersburg, and the spring at my chateau in Corfu, where I had the advantage of perfect quiet to mourn your loss. For the last two months I have been in Vienna; about a week ago, I received from my steward the letter in which you did me the honor to announce your resurrection, and at the same time your desire to see me. I at once paid my farewell calls, and here I am. Now," she added, " if you will permit me to remove the dust of my journey, I shall have no wish unfulfilled."

" I will conduct you to your apartment," said my uncle.

" Nephew," she said, making me a courtesy, " be prepared to humor my caprices; I have many of them, I assure you. Your turn will come."

They left the room, and I remained astonished at their mutual accord. You understand already the effect produced upon me by my aunt, and I was none the less surprised at my uncle. A complete change seemed to have taken place in him; he no longer swore; his manners and language were those of the best society, unconstrained, unembarrassed, and so natural, that it showed he must have had great experience in the most refined circles. He never tripped once. He was another man, and it was evident that this man was the only one my aunt Eudoxie de Cornalis had ever known.

" Well, what do you think of your aunt?" he asked me on his return in about five minutes.

" I am delighted with her, uncle; she is as charming as possible."

" Did you expect to see a fright?" he exclaimed.

" Certainly not!" I answered. " But my aunt might have been Venus herself without possessing the character and intelligence which I suspect she does."

" Oh, you can scarcely judge of her yet," he replied, carelessly. " You will see later; she is a thorough woman."

My aunt did not appear again till breakfast time.
Her entrance was like a burst of sunshine in the dining-
room, ordinarily occupied by only my uncle and myself.
My uncle surely felt the same impression as myself, for,
leaning toward me, he whispered:

"Don't you see, already, how she ornaments the
house?"

My aunt seated herself, and while removing her gloves,
glanced at the table, the dishes, the servants, and the
arrangement of the room.

"François," she said to my uncle's old valet, "send
me the gardener at four o'clock, please."

"Yes, madame."

"And the steward, also."

"I am the steward," said my uncle.

"Indeed! allow me to congratulate you. I ought to
have guessed it."

"It seems to me, though, that I have failed in something: Does not this new furniture please you?"

"On the contrary, it is very handsome, and I recognize your exquisite taste; but what are those big vases
doing there, with their immense mouths open to catch
the dust?"

"Those mandarins," said my uncle, "were presented to
me by the Emperor of China."

"Oh! you men! you men!" exclaimed my aunt,
laughing. "If you were in Paradise, you would forget
to contemplate the Eternal! But captain, my lord and
my master, what is the use of having conservatories full
of flowers if you never enjoy them?"

The breakfast passed off delightfully. My aunt gave
orders to François with a foresight which a woman alone
knows how to employ, and as if by enchantment, my

uncle found everything at his hand; before he had time
to ask for wine, his glass was filled. We had never been
so well served before.

After breakfast, my aunt proposed taking a walk in the
park. She took my arm and we set forth. I will not
bore you with an account of our stroll, during which my
aunt and I became very well acquainted. With supreme
tact and with no appearance of effort, at the end of a
quarter of an hour, by discreet questioning, she had made
me tell her all my affairs from a to z, my studies, my
tastes, even my youthful follies, which more than once
made her smile. I need not tell you, however, that I
said . nothing about my life as a pacha. My uncle
walked by us and did not interrupt our conversation.
During our walk we passed the path which led to the
Turkish pavilion.

"Oh! let us go to El-Nouzha," said my aunt.

At these words I cast a look of distress at my uncle;
he did not move a muscle.

"The gate is closed up," he said; "Kasre-el-Nouzha
is let!"

"Let!" she cried. "To whom?"

"To a great personage, a friend of mine from Constantinople, Mohammed-Aziz; you do not know him."

She did not insist, and you can imagine that I breathed
again.

After an hour's walk in the park, aunt Eudoxie had
achieved my conquest. However, although everything about her excited my curiosity, I asked her very
few questions, not wishing to show my ignorance in
regard to her, a strange situation for a nephew. She
appeared disposed to talk freely with me, though, and to
treat me as an intimate friend. What surprised me the

most was the attitude of my uncle, who had spoken to
me no more of her than he had of my aunt Cora of the
Grands-Palmiers. They seemed as affectionate as possible; they chatted of the past, and I discovered that the
bonds between them had never been broken, despite
the Mohammedan proceedings of my uncle, of which,
however, she seemed indeed to have no suspicion. I
learned that she had accompanied him on many of his
voyages, and that, two years before, he had lived with
her for six months at Corfu. As for him, he talked with
her so simply and innocently that I came to the conclusion that he must be quite as happy in his other marriages, and he would have been no more embarrassed
with my aunt Van Cloth, if by chance she had appeared.

When we returned to the chateau, my aunt asked me
to post some letters for her. I went to her room to get
them; she had written some half dozen to different
countries, and while she was sealing them, I examined
the thousand-and-one objects with which she had adorned
her boudoir; flowers in vases, books and albums upon
the table; upon the mantelpiece, some pictures on little
gilded easels, among them a beautiful miniature of a
young and handsome man in a Turkish costume embroidered with gold, and with a fez ornamented with an
aigrette of precious stones upon his head.

"Do you recognize that gentleman?" asked my aunt,
as I took it up to examine it closer.

"What?" I cried. "Can it be my uncle?"

"Himself; in his robes of Grand Mamamouchi; that is
a great rarity, for you know he has Turkish ideas in
regard to never having his likeness taken."

"That is indeed true!" I said. "This is the first
portrait of him I have ever seen."

"I have every reason to believe it is the only one in existence; that was the most troublesome victory I ever won over him."

We then talked of my uncle, of his peculiarities and his many excellent qualities. She told me certain events in his life which quite equaled the legends of some mythological hero; among other things, the story of their marriage, which, abbreviated, is as follows:

My aunt, the descendant of one of the noblest and wealthiest Greek families, inhabited with her father a castle in Thessaly, a country in part Mohammedan. During the festival of Baïram, the Turks began a massacre of the Christians, which lasted three days. Several families took refuge in a church, barricaded the doors and defended themselves desperately with the aid of their servants. The assassins had already broken down the door of the sanctuary and all were about to be slain, when suddenly a man arrived at full gallop, followed by soldiers. He struck right and left with his scimiter, and forced a passage through the crowd. The Turks fled in dismay, and the Christians were saved. The horseman was my uncle, then in command of the province. The unfortunates who had been rescued from death crowded about him; the women and girls fell at his feet. My aunt was among them; she was then fifteen and as beautiful as the day. You can imagine the impression made upon her by the sight of her superb rescuer. My uncle on his side at once fell in love with so much beauty. As he had to judge and punish the rebels, he made his headquarters at the castle of the Cornalis. He had twenty men executed, and asked for Eudoxie's hand, which, despite his gratitude, her father refused to grant to a Turkish general. The lovers were in despair; they

separated, after exchanging vows of eternal love. After
three months of correspondence and secret interviews,
there were an elopement and a marriage. It was in consequence of this circumstance, that, converted by love,
and, moreover, in disgrace for having shown too much
clemency in favor of the Christians, my uncle quitted
for the last time the service of the sultan. The pardon
of the Cornalis followed; then also he obtained from the
Pope the title of Count of the Holy Empire.

All this will explain to you how it is that my aunt,
heiress to a great property, possesses in her own right a
large fortune.

CHAPTER XI.

I have had scarcely any time to write you, my dear
Louis. We have lived a quiet, domestic life for the last
two weeks, and during those two weeks Férouzat has
been entirely transformed. My aunt is certainly very
ornamental, as my uncle said, and she is the life of the
house. Her presence has naturally introduced into our
circle of friends a certain etiquette, which, however, has
nothing stiff or constrained about it. As might have been
foretold, the Countess de Monteclaro, who was formerly
very intimate with Dr. Morand, could not fail to become
great friends with Mademoiselle Genevieve; the result is
that Mademoiselle Genevieve and the children pass
almost every day at the chateau. In the evening we have
parties, to which all the youthful element of the neighborhood are invited; my aunt, who is an excellent musician,
organizes little concerts, and sometimes we end up with
a dance.

All this is of advantage to me in analyzing my Oriental life, which is enveloped more than ever in the greatest mystery. I have invented an important botanical work upon the *flora* of Provence as an excuse for my daily excursions, which naturally have as an object El-Nouzha. It is known, however, that I sometimes visit His Excellency Mohammed-Aziz, but with the respect which his misfortunes command. No one concerns himself with the exiled minister; it is recognized that " he shuts himself up like a bear," and he is left to himself.

My aunt is decidedly a charming woman. Nothing could be more delightful than the conversations I have with her; she is at once a sort of a mother and a comrade to me. The memory of the child she used to dandle on her knees has never been effaced from her mind, and although since that time I had almost forgotten her existence, my affection to-day is none the less very sincere; then, besides, brought up in schools and at college, I thoroughly enjoy the home-life which up to now I never knew.

As you may suppose, my aunt is acquainted with my uncle's plans for me; she knows his god-daughter, Anna Campbell, and she tells me she is charming. She sometimes rallies my uncle on this relationship, pretending that the captain has returned to the bosom of the church, without suspecting it. Thus taken care of, I live my life as I wish, sometimes passing the whole day in the library. I ought to add, however, that my aunt, who is not easily deceived, comments in her own fashion on my frequent absences from the chateau.

" André," she said to me the other day, laughingly, " tell me about your *botany*. Is she blonde or brunette?"
" Blonde, aunt," I answered, laughing also.

In the midst of all this, the pacha, like an Olympian god, goes on his way with the calmness which never deserts him. Two days ago, Rabassu, his lieutenant, appeared—Rabassu, whom my uncle calls "the author of his death." He has just brought the " Belle-Virginie " from Zanzibar with a cargo of cinnamon, for we carry on, you know, or, rather, I carry on a trade in spices. Rabassu, on his return to Toulon, learned of the resurrection of Barbassou-Pacha, and he hastened sheepishly here and positively trembled when he met the captain, at thought of the blast awaiting him; but at his first faltering words of explanation, my uncle interrupted him with a friendly slap on the back, and contented himself with rallying him on his childish credulity. However, his appearance brought up the affair of the camels again. Where are they? The captain promised them to the Zoological Gardens at Marseilles; his honor is engaged, and he wishes them to be found. I agree with him, for my inheritance is incomplete without them. Very pressing letters have been sent to his friend Picklock, and to the commander of Aden. If necessary, an appeal will be made to England. She is evidently responsible.

In my next epistle, I will tell you what the news is at El-Nouzha. Since I suspended that side of my interesting history, there has been some progress among my houris in their education. We walk upon roses.

CHAPTER XII.

There is no doubt about it, my friend, the Turks are calumniated. We say and believe that these turbaned people wallow in materialism, and are not civilized. Abso-

lute and confident in a singular infatuation for our ideas,
our customs, and ourselves, we settle, by sovereign
decisions, the highest questions of sentiment. The tourna-
ments and the courts of love of the Middle Ages have
regulated the way the perfect lover should worship his
lady-love. We have even succeeded in having this
belief accepted, that the French chevalier was the para-
gon of elegance in love, and the type of gallant grace.

However, you will acknowledge, I hope, that these
foolish ideas are not quite correct. That we know how
to love is no great matter. With us philosophers, the
chief thing is to know if our ideal is the superior ideal.
Is our worship for woman more worthy of her and of us
than the entirely pagan worship of Oriental nations?
Here rises at once the primordial question: Polygamy or
monogamy? Both institutions the result of human and
divine laws, both inscribed and defined in the codes of
morality and in holy books. The one, taking its source
in the Bible, and remaining faithful to its traditions; the
other, born from the simple conditions of a new society.
Although our pride forces us to admit the superiority of
our time-honored civilization, we must not conclude that
we alone possess the absolutely true notion. It all
depends upon place, customs, and time. Was not
Jacob, marrying at the same time Leah and Rachel, the
two daughters of Laban, much nearer the primitive sentiment of natural and revealed law than ourselves?
Would you dare to blame him because, yielding to the
supplications of his beloved Rachel, he also espoused his
maid-servant, Bilhah, for the sole purpose of giving himself a son? In presence of that idyl of the patriarchal
age, what becomes of our theories, our ideas, our prejudices, the fruits of a vain education?

You will certainly not do me the injury of believing that, unsteady in my beliefs, I dream of deserting the principles in which I was born. But a study so serious as the one to which I have devoted myself, demands the most sincere and loyal examination. I do not judge, I simply state the case. In point of fact, it is certain that even in our days, the people whose laws allow of a plurality of wives are much more numerous than monogamous people. Statistics show that, out of a billion of the earth's inhabitants, Christianity, in all its branches and including Judaism, only comprises two hundred and sixty million souls, according to Balbi; two hundred and forty millions, according to the Biblical Society of London. The rest are Mohammedans, Buddhists, Idolaters, etc., all more or less practicing polygamy. The result is that on our terrestrial globe, the monogamists are only in the proportion of one to three. This is the real truth.

Are we wrong? Are they right? To decide upon this point is not my affair. Philosophers and theologians, wiser than I, have exhausted themselves in the effort to determine it. Voltaire has very adroitly settled the question in his own manner, by supposing that an imaginary deity had decreed this original inequality of situation, saying:

"I will draw a line from the Caucasus Mountains to Egypt, and from Egypt to the Atlas Mountains; all those who live to the east of this line may marry many wives; those who live to the west of it shall have but one."

And, in fact, that is the state of the case.

But this important point settled, there remains a much higher question to be elucidated, that of sentiment. The worship of woman being our only object, it must be decided on which side of the line this worship is the most sacred, the most worthy of, and the most flattering for, her. Surely, our dogma is the purer, our law the more divine. However, as honest judges, we ought to examine, perhaps, if we do not derogate from our fixed principles. And I acknowledge that it is not without some embarrassment that I enter upon this delicate point. Before every court of law, polygamy is a punishable crime. But can it not be said that in practice the court knows that the law is not observed? What is this monogamy of which we boast so loudly? What is it except the license of a tolerated depravity to the profit of an ideal virtue? But look at the fatal consequences of this hypocrisy. What becomes of the illusions and dreams of our youth in the *liaisons* which are the result of our manners and customs, and from whence one departs at thirty a skeptic and with both heart and soul defiled? What is the result, except contempt for woman and doubt of all virtue?

With the Turks, illegitimate love not existing, woman is an object of absolute respect. Never having but one master, and purchased as a slave, she becomes a wife the moment she enters the harem. Her rights are sacred; she can not be abandoned. The laws protect her; she has a recognized position, a title, her children are legitimate, and if, perchance ——

I interrupt this philosophical digression to tell you of an important event. El-Nouzha has become the stage of a most stirring drama. A revolt is declared among my sultanas.

CHAPTER XIII.

Whence came this thunderbolt from a clear sky, at the very moment I was congratulating myself on my calm and peaceful life? It is only possible to understand it by relating to you the little details which the changes at Férouzat made me neglect.

You have not forgotten, I think, the terrible alarm into which my harem was thrown by the news of my uncle's resurrection. That day of fright and anguish was truly a very cruel one for my poor houris, who expected some terrible Turkish tragedy. Their terrors dissipated, they were more fascinating than ever. But, unfortunately, one little detail, apparently insignificant, of that day gradually caused a disturbance in the harmony, which up to that time had been so perfect, and excited jealousies. Kondjé-Gul had gone to the chateau, and a foolish desire to attempt a like escapade took possession of Nazli and Zouhra. I declared my formal opposition, and the childish longing naturally changed into a fixed idea from the moment it encountered an obstacle. Their imaginations, owing to the restricted circle of their thoughts, became inflamed with curiosity. The forbidden fruit attracted them. In short, seeing their sorrow, which was increased still more by a thousand jealous suspicions of a preference for Kondjé-Gul, I had almost resolved to yield once, when my aunt's arrival cut short any thought of weakness.

I then considered that I was armed with an unanswerable reason for refusing, but I found myself wofully mistaken. On learning that my uncle's wife was at the

chateau, they demanded ·to make her acquaintance.
According to Turkish custom, they were even obliged,
as *cadines*, to make a visit to my uncle's wife, "whom her
title of legitimate spouse placed hierarchically above
them." I got out of the difficulty by saying that my
aunt, being a Christian, her faith forbade her to have
anything to do with Mohammedans.

My friend, what particularly distinguishes the Turkish
woman from the woman improved by our remarkable
civilization, is the instinctive, innate respect which she
always keeps for man. Man is the master; the lord.
She is his servant; and such an idea as that she is his
equal never occurs to her. The Koran, upon this point,
has scarcely altered the Biblical tradition. Unfortunately, I confess, I have changed in my household the
Mussulman law. Imbued with a higher ideal, you will
comprehend without my telling you, that my first care
was to abolish the slavery of the harem, by inculcating
in my houris principles in conformity with my title of
Christian. I wished, like a second Prometheus, to ani-
mate with the divine spark those young and beautiful
barbarians, still in the darkness of their Oriental superstitions. I wished to elevate their souls; to cultivate
their minds. In short, to make them my companions
and no longer helots.

I can proclaim with pride that I partially succeeded
in my task. After three months of this system all trace
of the yoke had disappeared. With that gift of metamorphosis which woman possesses and which we never
possess, thanks above all to the revelations as to our
manners and customs depicted in novels selected by me
and read to them by Kondjé-Gul during my absence,
and to which they listened with open ears—eager to

know everything of that world of which they were ignorant—I soon obtained charming results. The odd mixture of sultanic graces harmonizing with our civilized
graces, the ingenuous ignorance and intuitions of
coquetry, the Eastern fascination striving with modest
reserve, all this formed the most ravishing subject of
study ever offered to philosopher. However, I must
acknowledge that the education of their intelligence did
not keep pace with the cultivation of their souls, and often
exposed them to many solecisms. It was, besides, for
my interest to keep them in a certain ignorance of the
absolute laws of our world. Imbued with their native
beliefs, they credulously accepted without hesitation
whatever I pleased to tell them as to "the customs of
harems in France," and they conformed to them without
asking to know more. There resulted none the less
in their minds principles of independence and will which
were produced with the elevation of their sentiments.
This notion of a tenderer and a truer love was henceforth an arm against my absolute authority. Happy to
be a lover rather than a master, I lost nothing by it.
Love was kept alive by those thousand pretty little strat-
agems of a woman who loves. On their side, having no
other ambition, no other thought than to please me as
the sole object of their common flame, each of them
strove to gain some advantage over her rivals—an emu-
lation in which I delighted. However, although I shared
my tenderness with rare equity, I could not always avoid
jealous quarrels between them. Then there were sadness,
tender reproaches, and tears, followed by reconciliation
and foolish gayety. But you do not know what it is to
keep in the concord of a perfect household those vari-
able, excitable imaginations, which mingled their super-

stitions with the higher ideas I had striven to inculcate
in them, and which they often misinterpreted. All this
made the most charming originality. My little animals
became women, and with the sentiment of a more intelligent love, I saw also appear mutinous caprices at the
least suspicion of any preference with which they thought
they could accuse me.

I must tell you that Kondjé-Gul, who is really very
intelligent, applied herself to her studies with much
ardor, and it naturally followed that she soon surpassed
her companions. This superiority had already excited
their envy, which was increased by the famous escapade
to the chateau, of which the foolish girl told them marvelous tales. I should add, also, that Kondjé-Gul, excessively jealous, at times was the cause of stormy scenes.
Hadidjé, I don't know why, particularly excited her
fears. Hadidjé is very hot-headed, and the result was a
constant coolness between them. But these were only
passing clouds in an otherwise azure sky. For the passiveness of the harem I had substituted love; for obedience, freedom.

However, my houris preserved too much the instincts
of their race not to be elated, like children, at their new
position. Equal in all their rights, they pretended to
exactly the same rank. So it happened that Hadidjé,
Nazli, and Zouhra at last took umbrage at Kondjé-Gul.
Kondjé-Gul was wrong in trying to surpass them.
Kondjé-Gul, they said, set herself up as wiser than they.
Kondjé-Gul took the airs of a favorite. I must confess
that the coquette tried only too much to make them feel
her advantages, of which she was decidedly proud. One
evening she sat down at the piano, and negligently
played a short waltz, which she had learned in secret to

surprise me. You can imagine the effect. Her triumph
excited the others to the greatest extent, and they
pouted for the rest of the evening. Finally, one day,
on my arrival at the harem, I found Kondjé-Gul shut up
in her room in tears. The storm, for a long time suspended, had burst upon her haughty head—Hadidjé,
Zouhra, and Nazli had beaten her.

I patched up a peace by means of a new declaration
of principles, and effected a reconciliation between
them; but a faction was born. At the moment when I
least expected it, Hadidjé, Nazli, and Zouhra returned
to the idea of going in secret to the chateau. This
project, always a favorite one, which hitherto had only
been spoken of in detachments, they now pursued in a
body, combining their forces with rare skill and prudence. Their arms were tenderness and those thousand
little womanly cajoleries which make us almost always
yield, conquered, to the most unjust wishes. My path-
way was still strewn with flowers, but the trap was
sprung under the blossoms. At the end of a few weeks,
when I was well caught in their cunning net, their tac-
tics suddenly changed; I no longer heard a word of
Férouzat, but I was met with frivolous caprices, sudden
sullenness, unexpected refusals—my odalisques were
civilized.

I was too good a tactician to allow myself to be caught
by this game, which I pretended not to notice. At the
slightest success which they seemed to win over me, I at
once turned my attentions to Kondjé-Gul, and the faction disbanded and threw themselves immediately upon
my mercy. Unfortunately, Kondjé-Gul, confident in my
weakness for her, conceived ·the idea of gaining a decisive victory at one bold stroke. A few evenings ago,

when she had accompanied me to the secret door, she suddenly threw it open, laughing, and started toward the chateau across the park of Férouzat. I darted after her and soon overtook her, embarrassed as she was by her slippers and her trailing robe. I brought her back to the harem, where the others awaited, in the greatest excitement, the result of such an audacious attempt. I learned that she had boasted that she would obtain over them this new triumph. After such an act of revolt, I was forced to make an example of her; I was very severe, and a terrible scene ensued. Kondjé-Gul had too much pride to humiliate herself before her rivals, who rejoiced at her defeat. Angry and out of temper, she ruined all our former peace; for three days she remained haughty, arrogant, accepting her disgrace without deigning to take a step toward reconciliation. I need not tell you that Nazli, Hadidjé, and Zouhra redoubled their tenderness and attentions.

Things were in this state when the great event I have undertaken to narrate to you occurred.

The other evening I was at the harem; Nazli and Zouhra were playing Turkish airs upon the zither, while Hadidjé, seated at my feet, her head leaning upon her clasped hands, hummed the words of each melody. Kondjé-Gul, cold and dignified, in the attitude at once provoking and resigned of a hardened rebel, was smoking a cigarette upon the veranda; but the furtive glances which she cast at Hadidjé showed that her calmness was affected. Since the evening before, we had not exchanged a word. She was attired to-night with the greatest splendor, as if to force me to contemplate the beauties of my lost paradise; her beautiful golden hair, in long tresses, flowed a little in disorder from under the cap, embroidered with pearls. She wore a large gauze veil, in which she affected to envelope herself to hide her attractions from my profane gaze. Her lovely face wore a resolute and mutinous expression, like an irritated Venus. She had blackened her eyes, which I had forbidden, and lengthened her eyebrows, which joined in the Turkish fashion. The criminal was adorably pretty.

You see the picture and you divine the state of my mind. The strange sounds of the zither, its penetrating and singularly melancholy vibrations; the odd, graceful costumes; the *salon* full of the odor of the flowers with which the daughters of the Orient are always adorned; finally, the rebel herself, solemn and jealous, in a corner of the window; all this kept me in a sort of dreamy beatitude, which I can not describe, but which you can understand.

By-and-by the music ceased.

"André," said Hadidjé, "would you like to go out into the garden?"

"Come!" I said, rising.

She took my arm; Zouhra and Nazli followed us.

As we crossed the veranda I passed near Kondjé-Gul; with a movement of superb disdain, she drew back a little, as if fearful of my touching her robe. And, with a look of contempt at Hadidjé, she drew her veil across her face and leaned against the balustrade, watching us depart. The evening was a beautiful one in autumn; the air soft, and the skies clear and starry. The dry leaves rustled under our feet. Hadidjé wanted to go for a row and we went toward the lake. From the boat, through the leaves of the trees, we could see Kondjé-

Gul, her figure outlined like a solitary silhouette against the illuminated window of the *salon*.

"I am glad of it," said Hadidjé, who was rowing with Nazli. "She is awfully lonely. Why did she pretend to have more privileges than we? Let us stay here."

"Oh!" said Zouhra, who was reclining upon a pile of cushions, "not all the evening. It is a little chilly."

"Why didn't you bring your *feridjié;* you are always cold?" said Nazli.

"I will go for it if you like," said I to Zouhra.

"Oh! no!" she answered quickly. "If you leave us we shall be afraid."

"I will go," said Hadidjé, who still held to her idea.

We rowed to a place nearer the chateau, and Hadidjé, none too brave herself, started off on the run.

"Keep your eyes on me all the time, won't you," she said, gathering up her long train.

We saw her reach the veranda in safety. She mounted the steps and passed before Kondjé-Gul. It seemed to us that Kondjé-Gul addressed her vehemently and that she answered in the same manner. Finally, they both entered the house, and then suddenly we heard piercing cries. Fearing some encounter between the two jealous girls, I ran toward the chateau followed at a distance by Nazli and Zouhra, trembling at being left alone. On entering I found Hadidjé and Kondjé-Gul, their hair in disorder and their garments torn, in a fierce strug-gle with one another. Kondjé-Gul was armed with a small gold poignard, which she had worn in her hair, and she struck Hadidjé with it. When she caught sight of me, she fled and locked herself in her chamber.

We pressed about Hadidjé, who was bleeding from a wound in the shoulder. Fortunately, the weapon,

inoffensive to make a serious wound, had not penetrated
the flesh; but, broken off by the blow, it had made a
long ugly scratch. I stopped her cries, but not without
an effort; Mohammed and the servants came running in;
I sent them all away, and having calmed Nazli and
Zouhra, I bathed the wound with water. After a few
minutes, Hadidjé, who had thought herself killed, recovered her coolness and began to complain bitterly of her
treatment. I questioned her, and she told us that when
she entered the *salon* to get a *feridjié* Kondjé-Gul followed
her and with the utmost violence, accused her of being the
cause of her disgrace, reproaching her with hypocritical
maneuvers to engross me. Hadidjé, according to her
version, had answered only with extreme sweetness, when
suddenly Kondjé-Gul, exasperated, attacked her with
her dagger.

I knew Hadidjé's character too well to credit all her
story, but it was important to put a stop to such out-
breaks. The happiness of my household, hitherto so
peaceful, was compromised if I did not act like a just
and severe husband. After the attack of Kondjé-Gul,
my houris angrily demanded a terrible vengeance and
asked me to deliver her at once to the cadi. I had great
difficulty in appeasing their harshness ; but finally they
agreed to a less tragic punishment, but insisted on her
expulsion from the harem and that she should be sent
back to Turkey.

I promised to satisfy their wrongs, and leaving Hadidjé
to the care of Zouhra and Nazli, I declared that I would
go at once and interrogate the criminal, after which I
would pronounce sentence.

Kondjé-Gul was shut up in her own room. I found
her seated upon a divan, the cushions of which seemed

to have been rumpled and crushed in an access of despair
and rage; her attitude was despairing, her look sombre,
and her hands clasped tightly together. Her face and
neck bore the traces of Hadidjé's nails. The black about
her eyes was washed down upon and besmirched her
cheeks. She had the air of a little savage with the grace
of a child.

She did not stir at my entrance; I walked up to her
and said with the solemn accent of a judge:

"Unhappy girl, what have you done?"

She kept silent and remained motionless, her eyes fixed
upon the carpet.

"After such an action, have you nothing to say?" I
continued.

"Why do you love her?" she said at last in a fierce
tone.

"And why should I love you," I replied, "when your
wickedness and your jealousy led you into disobedience
and crime? when you excite among us quarrels and
discord?"

At these reproaches she suddenly sprang up.

"Then you do not love me?" she cried.

"This is no time to answer you. I demand an account
of the action you have committed."

"Very well, if you do not love me, I want you to avow
it and I will die. What have I done that you should
prefer Hadidjé to me? She is more beautiful than I,
perhaps? If you think me ugly," she added with the
accent of concentrated despair, "tell me so, and I will
throw myself into the lake and you shall never see me
again!"

"No, I do not say that," I answered, hoping to calm
her.

"Then what have you to reproach me with? Hadidjé loves you better than I do, perhaps?"

"There is no question of Hadidjé's sentiments or of mine. We are speaking of your violence, of the blow you struck her with your poignard."

"Why did she tell me you loved her better than me?" she responded.

"She told you that?"

"Yes! And she pretends that you swore it. I do not wish to be loved like a slave. I have learned in your books that the women of your country die when they are no longer loved; if you have ceased to love me, I wish to die! You have told me that I have a heart, a soul, an intelligence like them, and that a woman's love makes her the equal of her master. Do you dare to say, ingrate, that I do not love you? Have I ever been jealous of Zouhra, or of Nazli? Why should that Hadidjé be everything to you? If you care no longer for me," she added with a burst of tears, "well! cut my hair, shave my eyebrows, and send me down among the servants!"

Saying these words, she cast herself, half delirious at my feet; the tears rolled down her cheeks and upon my hands which she covered with kisses. She showed such poignant distress, that, although decided to punish, I felt softened in spite of myself. In presence of a passionate excitement which could think of nothing except its own jealous fury, I saw that I should try in vain to awaken in her any consciousness of her wrong-doing. She would not listen; she felt nothing except the cry of her own sorrow; I did not love her, and I loved Hadidjé! These words broke forth again and again from her lips with such convulsive sobs, that, moved with pity and forgetting my resolution, I could not refrain from a word of protest. Scarcely was it pronounced when she cried:

"Is that true? You love me! Will you swear it?"

I saw my imprudence, but it was too late. Kondjé-Gul, passing from affliction to joy, clasped me in her arms. I tried to remain severe; but how could I reason with her foolish jealousy? She would not listen; she implored me, besought me to say once more I loved her. After a time I thought I had finally brought her to realize our situation and the just causes of complaint I had against her for her conduct.

"Well! yes," she said, "I was foolish; three days ago I ought to have thrown myself at your feet. If you knew how unhappy I was at your coldness! Why, when you came in just now, believing that I had lost you forever, I was thinking how I should kill myself. But you have forgiven me, haven't you? No, don't speak to me of them!" she continued quickly, seeing that I was about to answer her.

"You know very well that I am no longer like them; you have formed my heart for another love than that of the harem. I no longer love you in the way they do! But you, you shall love me as you like, as your servant, if that is your will. Lock me up, punish me! I ask nothing except to see you, except to love you. Yes, I was wrong to strike that Hadidjé; you know that I am still a savage, you have often told me so. Well! Teach me your ideas, your religion! Tell me, what do you wish me to be?" she added in such a sweet, tender voice that I was entirely conquered.

I was astonished at her words, at her impassioned elo-quence, which I had never suspected, and which I heard now from her lips for the first time. The butterfly of her soul had opened its wings. Psyche was awakened to love! No more that vague passive love of the senses, but the love of the heart, which is life, with its sufferings, its joys, its pains. I contemplated her in surprise, attracted by some indefinable new charm.

Louis, what shall I say to you? An hour after having entered Kondjé-Gul's room, our quarrel, her jealousy, her crime, the proposed punishment, were all forgotten.

However, after I reached a more exact appreciation of my defeat, I could not conceal from myself the embarrassment which would result from my strange conduct. It would appear very odd to my wives to let them know that the violent scene and the blow received by poor Hadidjé had become precisely a cause of reconciliation. How should I appear before the victim to whom I had promised justice? It was impossible to show such a disdain of *fas* and *nefas*, by granting to the fault such an incredible pardon. What would Nazli and Zouhra say? It would be all over with my authority, my character!

It was necessary, therefore, at all costs, to hide my imprudent weakness until their anger should be appeased, or until an apology from Kondjé-Gul to Hadidjé should be the excuse for pardon. But at the first words I spoke to call her to reason, Kondjé-Gul, full of pride at having conquered me, would not listen to a word in regard to her humiliating herself before her rival. In vain I represented to her that my dignity, propriety, and justice were at stake. She held to her victory and would relinquish none of her advantages. Finally, however, she understood the gravity of the situation. "Well," she said, "this is what we will do, and it will be very nice. Let them believe that you have scolded me dreadfully—and

that is very true, for you were very naughty when you
first came in."

"You didn't deserve it, perhaps?" I answered.

"Hush! Be still!" she said, with a little grimace, putting her finger to my lips. "You are going to begin
again. Let me tell you my plan, which will arrange all."

"What is your plan?"

"Well, you must tell them that you were inexorable,
and that you treated me like an odious creature. I shall
pretend to be more angry than ever against you. Before
them, we won't notice each other. We will make them
believe that all is finally ended between us; that you
have decided to send me away to have me sold."

"What an idea!" I exclaimed.

"Please do. It will be so charming to have a secret
with you. And then it will seem to me that I am loved
more than they."

"Because we deceive them, I suppose."

"Well, yes," she cried, laughing; "because we deceive
them! Besides," she added, in a tone of conviction, "you
understand very well, yourself, that we could not act
otherwise. And, I declare to you, I will never, *never*,
ask pardon of that wretched Hadidjé!"

I was forced to accept for the time being this compromise, which at all events satisfied apparently the demands
of propriety. On leaving Kondjé-Gul, I prudently
returned at once to the chateau, for fear of awakening the
suspicions of my wives.

However, I must confess it was not without some
apprehensions that I came the next day to the harem. But
I was soon reassured at seeing the amiability which
reigned among my houris. The absence of Kondjé-Gul,
who remained stoically shut up in her apartment, left

them no doubt as to her complete disgrace and her certain expulsion. I even learned that, showing some black-
and-blue marks which she had made herself, the madcap
had told Nazli that I had beaten her. Hadidjé, a little
proud of her injury, continued to assume an interesting
air, in her position as chief heroine of this terrible tragedy. In reality it was only a scratch which caused her
very little suffering. After the storms of the last few
days the morning passed like an idyl. Harmony was in
all hearts. I left them convinced that, after the way in
which I had accomplished my great act of justice, they
had nothing more to fear from a rival.

Satisfied at this happy outcome, and relieved from all
anxiety, I returned to the chateau, when, as I was passing through a grove of trees, Kondjé-Gul suddenly
sprang out and threw herself into my arms.

"What! You here?" I exclaimed.

"Yes; I wished to see you," she cried, exulting with
joy like a child, "and then to hear you say that you love
me always."

"You silly girl! If you should be seen!"

"I don't care!" she said. "I jumped out of my window; they think me a prisoner. I glided under the
veranda, so as not to be seen by Mohammed, and I came
here to watch for you. Now, don't scold. Now that I
have seen you I will return for fear of making your
wives suspicious. Tell me that I have done right."

Then, as she ran away:

"And you be prudent!" she added, in an important
tone.

CHAPTER XIV.

Eight days have passed since the dramatic events with their singular ending which I have narrated to you. Here I am, playing a false part in my household. I have a secret flirtation with one of my wives. Kondjé-Gul, pretending coldness, accentuates her rôle with melancholy affectations mingled with haughty disdain, and the madcap is delighted with the situation. After remaining shut up for two or three days she reappeared. She talks cynically of her approaching departure, and rejoices over it. We treat each other like a husband and wife definitely divorced, who, nevertheless, like well-bred people, pay each other a last tribute of strict politeness, after having irreparably disagreed. Hadidjé, Zouhra, and Nazli, confident in a victory which appears to them assured, admire the great justice of my character.

My dear Louis, must I confess to you the strangest result of this affair? Yes? I have promised you that this psychological study should be sincere and that nothing should be glossed over. Well, in my observations as an analyst, this mystery with Kondjé-Gul, this savor of forbidden fruit, is the most delightful thing I have discovered. Say, if you like, that I am a Pandour, a man perverted by the experiences of unbridled epicureanism; say that the attraction of dissimulation, of falsehood, this connivance like a childish concealment, possesses for my *blasé* heart a certain excitement; and, perhaps, you will not be far from the truth. You do not exact, I suppose, that I shall make excuses for a weak-

7

ness of this kind. I divine your thought. Despite my
display of principles, with an apparent contempt for that
strict duty, which I had prescribed for myself, of an
equal sharing of my heart among my household, I have
all the appearance of having made choice of a favorite?
Have I indeed done so? I don't know. What is the
use, besides, of finding fault with myself? Is tranquil
possession the narcotic of love? Does restraint, on the
other hand, serve as a spur? Without reasoning on the
inconsequence of humanity, it appears to me much more
simple to recognize, like Kondjé-Gul, in the present state
of affairs a decree of Fate. Would you dare to blame
me for sacrificing vain theories to the superior interest
which guides me? The fact of the matter is, that this
necessity for dissimulation, these pretenses, these clan-
destine rendezvous have given birth to the most delightful relations between Kondjé-Gul and myself. You
should see us, both playing a part in the presence of *the
others*. What maneuvers to exchange furtively some
smile, a secret pressure of the hand—what pretty airs of
disdain she knows how to assume for the benefit of her
unsuspicious rivals! If we are by chance alone—

"Quick!" she cries. "Your wives are no longer here"
And she throws herself into my arms.

These words upon her lips reveal quite a novel order
of sentiments, a strange form of love, which could only
be produced by the education of the harem. Although
already civilized at heart, Kondjé-Gul, still backward in
her ideas and her traditions, takes no thought of my
other wives. She could not conceive my being reduced
to the destitution of a poor or avaricious man, by refusing the luxury of odalisques. In her eyes, Hadidjé,
Zouhra, and Nazli form part of my household; but she—

she has my heart in secret. "For her, I am unfaithful;
I scale her balcony when all the rest are asleep."

All this is senseless, you will say. Well, my dear fellow, happiness is composed only of those nothings the
charm of which often rests solely in our imaginations. In
these hidden interviews I have discovered in Kondjé-
Gul, who is certainly endowed with wonderful intelligence, a thousand graces which I had never even suspected before. Nothing could be odder or more charming than her slave-like love, still humble and fearful, and
seemingly bewildered by the reality of her dream. Her
Oriental ideas, her childish superstitions, mingled with
the vague notions which she has of our world and of a
truer ideal, form the most original contrast in her heart
and mind. She is like a bird suddenly surprised by the
knowledge that it has wings and that does not yet dare
to launch itself into space. Join to all this, the ardor of
a passion exalted, perhaps, by solitude or by the satisfaction of a victory obtained over her rivals, and, if you
blame my conduct, you will understand at least the fascinations which have precipitated my fall.

At Férouzat, there is great news; the camels are found!
A letter from Captain Picklock tells us of this fact. My
uncle is overjoyed; we think of taking a journey to
Marseilles to receive them.

My aunt has undertaken, without seeming to have
much to do with it, a great work of benevolence in connection with Dr. Morand. I must tell you that the doctor discovered here, some years ago, a hot spring of
chalybeate waters, whose effects have been really marvelous upon the few patients he has been able to attract
to this place. He wishes to establish a sort of hospital
for convalescents. My aunt has all at once decided that

she, my uncle, and I shall furnish the funds. A hundred thousand francs are more than sufficient for this modest establishment. Only, through sentiments of delicacy and to hide any appearance of ostentation, it has been arranged with the mayor and the *curé* that an appeal for subscriptions shall be made, to give to the work an appearance of general charity and to associate all the neighborhood in it. The result is that Férouzat has been honored with a call from the préfect, and that my aunt has organized the leading people round about into a committee. I am naturally her secretary and you may imagine that her activity does not allow me to be idle.

I assure you, there is in my aunt the stuff of a statesman.

CHAPTER XV.

My friend, an incident affecting public order, and of quite exceptional gravity, has cast me into a state of the greatest dismay.

The other morning, my aunt set out to attend to the famous work she has in hand.

"André," she said to me, "accompany me like a good nephew; I need you."

And so we entered the carriage, I thinking that we were bound to the doctor's, or to the Cambouliou's. When we turned out of the avenue, Bernard, the coachman, asked for his orders.

"To El-Nouzha," said my aunt.

"What!" I cried, "you are going to see Mohammed-Aziz?"

"Yes," she replied, "the name of His Excellency will

look well on our list; it will be like a guarantee of our friendly foreign relations."

"What are you thinking of?   A Mohammedan!"

"The charity of an infidel does not differ in its effects from the charity of a Christian."

"But he lives so retired that such a call will surprise him very much."

"You are intimate with him and will introduce me, nothing can be more proper; that is why I have brought you."

Nothing could be more proper, in fact; I was caught. I did not know what to say, fearing to arouse my clever aunt's suspicions. I saw that her real object was to satisfy a curiosity which she had experienced for a long time. How could I combat her wish? By what plausible pretext could I prevent her from making such a natural call? I was at my wits' end, and I had nothing more to hope for, except in Mohammed-Aziz's behavior and his poor French, which would at least render the conversation very difficult. The carriage proceeded on its way and my aunt was delighted. I succeeded well enough in concealing my anxiety. After all, the principal danger was avoided when my aunt presented herself at the public entrance of El-Nouzha. The *sélamlik* which Mohammed inhabits, and where we would be received, is, according to Turkish custom, totally separated from the harem, whose gardens can not be seen on that side.

At the end of a quarter of an hour, we arrived before His Excellency's house. The gates were closed, as usual. The footman descended and rang, but there was no answer. I felt a ray of hope for an instant; but at the third ring, ordered by my aunt, one of Mohamm

people, the Cerberus on that side, appeared at the door.

"His Excellency, Mohammed-Aziz is at home, is he not?" cried my aunt. "Announce to him a call from M. André de Peyradę."

Recognizing me in the carriage, Cerberus hesitated. He was about to open the gates for the carriage. I told him quickly to obey my aunt. To let Mohammed know of our arrival, would put him on his guard.

"There is no need of having the carriage enter," said my aunt; "we will cross the lawn on foot. Give me your hand and help me out. If His Excellency does not receive, I shall at least have had a glimpse of the park. What an idea of the captain's to let this place!"

She descended without more ado, and we entered. "Oh! the sycamores have become superb," she said. At this moment, we perceived Mohammed descending the steps and coming toward us.

The danger was imminent and nothing could save me now. I summoned up all my coolness. At a few steps from His Excellency, I dropped my aunt's hand and hastened to meet him.

"Listen," I said to him in a low voice, "that is my aunt. Be careful and let her suspect nothing." I then introduced them, speaking that famous patois that you know. Mohammed replied in the same idiom, with a fitting but rather obscure compliment, when my aunt suddenly answered him in the purest Turkish. I felt myself lost. A minute afterward, we were installed in the *salon* of the *sélamlik*. My aunt disclosed the object of her visit. I must say that that animal of a Mohammed played his rôle with the greatest gravity and dignity,

although with a little fearfulness, as if he felt, hovering in
the air, a vague souvenir of the beatings with which
doubtless my uncle had trained him.   I did not let him
out of my sight, and his eyes wandered from my aunt to
her nephew with an expression of distress.   Great drops
of perspiration appeared on his forehead.   Finally, at a
sign from me, he promised a generous subscription and
all seemed going well.

I breathed again, relieved from my anxiety, when my
aunt, as we were about to leave, most gracefully and
politely expressed a desire to call upon his daughters,
whose acquaintance she would be enchanted to make.

I felt the blood run cold in my veins.   To refuse the
entrée of the harem to a woman of my aunt's rank would
be an insult; she knew too well Mussulman customs to
make it possible to offer any opposition.   Mohammed,
still majestic, did not hesitate to answer by a bow of
delighted acquiescence, and without the least embarrassment, he rose, saying that he would tell them of the
honor.   I was a little reassured.   By the way in which
the fellow played his part, it was evident that it was not
the first time he had been called upon to save the situation.

"You would like to go with me, wouldn't you?" said
my aunt, laughing, when he had quitted us.

"Certainly, I would," I answered in a careless tone,
"but if his daughters resemble him, acknowledge that it
would be better not to dispel my illusions."

"You goose!"

Mohammed returned to say to my aunt that she was
expected, and preceding her with great ceremony, he
opened the doors communicating with the harem.   I was
left alone.   What was going to happen?   Although I

was already quieted by the incredible assurance of my
eunuch, the moment was critical. It was evident that
my houris would be in a great state of agitation. They
could chatter at their ease, as my aunt spoke Turkish,
and they might, perhaps, innocently betray all. If one of
them should pronounce my name, my aunt would know
everything.

I awaited in an uneasiness you can imagine. Finally,
after half an hour of torturing anxiety, the opening of a
door in the next room warned me that I was about to
know my fate. My aunt entered; I did not dare to look
at her. Fortunately, at the first words, I understood
that I had nothing to fear; she complimented Mohammed
on being so happy a father, promising to return often to
see his charming daughters, and we finally took leave of
His Excellency.

On our drive home, my aunt praised continually the
young Mussulmans, rallying me on my long, solitary
waiting, separated only by a wall from the pretty birds
imprisoned in their gilded cage. All during breakfast,
she regaled my uncle with the description of these
marvels of beauty. He regarded me out of the corner
of his eye with a furious air.

As soon as I could escape, I ran to El-Nouzha to
question Mohammed as to what had taken place in the
harem. He recounted to me the scene in its smallest
details. Nazli, Hadidjé, and Zouhra were alone when he
went to prepare them for my aunt's visit. Kondjé-Gul
was reading in her chamber and had not been summoned. At the news of so great an event, my houris
had uttered cries of joy. Mohammed, instructed by
my uncle never to forget his paternal character, was
obliged to recall to them, that, in consequence of the

peculiar customs in France, they must not let it be suspected that they knew me. They had promised all he
wished, swearing to observe all his commands. My aunt
was then introduced. At sight of her, my houris rose,
a little shy and timid, and conversation was commenced.
I need not tell you that the Countess de Monteclaro's
toilet was the principal topic.

I will not depict the excitement in which I found my
sultanas, nor the account they gave me in their turn of
this great event. Their vivid imaginations were already
occupied with the absolute necessity of returning my
aunt's call, whose grace had naturally so charmed them,
that they did not even imagine that there could be any
obstacle in the way of relations so pleasantly inaugu-
rated. In the evening they talked of nothing but the
incidents of that happy day, recalling, before Kondjé-
Gul, left out in the cold, and whom they by no means
intended to associate in their new life, all the pleasant
things the wife of the pacha had said to them. Poor
Kondjé-Gul, already in despair at having had no share
in the unexpected festivity, listened in silence, questioning me with startled eyes. I reassured her with a
gesture, allowing the foolish girls, who were overflowing
with gaiety, to form wonderful projects, which it would
have been useless to discuss.

I thought, on my side, of the necessary ending of this
unexpected complication. Although I had escaped this
time, the veil which covered the secrets of El-Nouzha
hung now only by a single thread; my aunt was not a
woman to be long deceived; the least imprudent word,
the slightest clue would awaken suspicion in her clever
mind. Curiosity lending its aid, I was not even sure
that she would not eagerly agree to an exchange of

relations with His Excellency's daughters; the very idea
made me tremble.

The result of my reflections was to take a decided
resolution to cut short the delicate situation. I had
been able, surrounding myself with the most profound
mystery, to lead at a few steps from the chateau my
Oriental life, so surely hidden behind the walls of El-
Nouzha. But after my aunt's visit, which had brought
her in contact with my houris, the commonest respect
for the proprieties forced me not to allow such a thing
to take place again. Our sojourn at Férouzat was,
moreover, drawing to an end, for we intended to pass the
winter in Paris. I resolved then to hasten our departure
and to remove my harem at once. Once lost in the noise
and crowd of the city, my secret would be safe.

The removal is decided. A conversation with my
uncle has simplified everything, for, as you may suppose,
I felt obliged to point out to him the danger of another
such an occurrence, which might perhaps cause my
aunt's eyes to be opened in regard to certain obscure
incidents in the captain's past. Barbassou-Pacha did not
seem much alarmed, but he approved my resolution,
and, scolding me a little, he gave me quite amiably the
help of his great experience. He has, or, rather, I have,
it appears, in Paris a hôtel which was built expressly for
His Excellency Mohammed-Aziz, when my uncle staid
in Paris; orders have already been given to have it put
in readiness. Plausible reasons for my taking a journey
have been invented; a pretended important business
matter, of which we have been talking for some days,
before my aunt, will " demand my presence." Indeed,
my uncle's *sang-froid* is wonderful.

At El-Nouzha, the prospects of a change have called

forth indescribable enthusiasm. The idea of seeing
Paris has inflamed all brains and caused the plan of
visiting Férouzat to be forgotten. To disarm all suspicion and conjecture, Mohammed will depart to-morrow,
ostensibly for Marseilles, as if he were returning to Turkey. As the cold weather is beginning, nothing could
be more natural than this return home, which, by a de-
tour, will end in the Faubourg Saint-Germain, where I
shall rejoin him next week.

CHAPTER XVI.

It is done! All has been executed without the least
hitch. I write to you from our hôtel in the Rue de
Varennes, Paris, where it seems to me that I have
returned after years of absence, so many events have
happened since I left here six months ago. All that
surrounds me is connected with a life of so long ago
that it is only with an effort that I can become accustomed to it now.

My harem is installed in the Rue de Monsieur, in a
superb hôtel whose gardens run down to the Boulevard
des Invalides. My uncle has, indeed, the tastes of an
ancient epicurean dropped by chance into our century.
The street is so quiet and almost deserted that you
might imagine yourself in a corner of aristocratic Versailles. My mystery is well hidden there. Mohammed,
in Paris, is no longer an exiled minister. He passes
quite modestly for a rich Turk with a taste for civilization;
he is called Omer-Rachid-Effendi, a name under which
he has already been here many times. My houris are
wonderstruck and their delight can not be described.

Naturally, the first thing to be done was to Europeanize
them. According to my orders, for as you understand
I do not appear in the matter, a fashionable dressmaker
was summoned by Mohammed. What an affair! The
danger was that their Oriental fascinations would be
rendered awkward or constrained by being all at once
imprisoned in the gehennas of civilization. By a happy
combination of fashion and fancy, the skillful artist has
invented for them toilets which are miracles of good taste
and simplicity. Nothing could be more successful than
this metamorphosis; the arrangement of the hair, above
all, completes it to such a point that I no longer recognize
my almehs under the coquettish little bonnet of our
Parisiennes. I repeat, it is a transfiguration full of surprise and unexpected attractiveness. In the costume of
our *élégantes*, their sparkling youth and eccentric beauty,
which I admired at El-Nouzha, appear full of new grace,
which the immediate comparison with women of our
world makes me appreciate all the more. In their civilized attire, the young foreigners are most distinguished
and piquant.

Once in Paris, naturally all is changed and their
existence is no longer to be passed between the four
walls of the harem. They are free at last to take walks
and make excursions; but here again is a most serious
question. To go into the streets, to the Champs Elysées,
to the Bois, with the face uncovered like infidels was alarming. They could not bring themselves to commit such an
immodest fracture of the Mussulman law, and I will confess to you that I felt, myself, an odd sort of shudder at the
thought. You see what I have come to! However,
to go out enveloped in their triple veils was not to be
thought of, as this would make them the object of

remarks. Finally, after much hesitation, Zouhra, the bravest, summoned up courage to go out with me, shut up in a coupé, and protected by a sort of very thick mantilla, which, after all, was scarcely less impenetrable than a *yashmak;* then, curiosity urging them and coquetry perhaps a little overcoming their modest instincts, they grew more bold, and one fine day they took a drive to the Bois, in a landau, with Mohammed. I mounted my horse and met them, without seeming to know them. All went well and they now drive out every day. Dressed as a European, Mohammed preserves an air of serene dignity, becoming a father taking his three daughters out for an airing. There is nothing, in fact, to attract unusual attention; if a black eye sparkles under the spotted veil, fashion permits the features to be sufficiently hidden to protect my sultanas' beauty from too bold looks.

Of course poor Kondjé-Gul, still tabooed, has no share in these amusements; but we gain from this some hours of liberty. On the second day, while my wives were at the Bois, we in our turn set out, arm in arm, like true lovers ; it was charming! We gained the boulevards on foot. You can divine her delight at each step. It was the first time she had gone out alone on my arm, the first time she felt free from the walls of the harem. As we passed, more than one curious person, struck by her sovereign attractions, stopped abruptly, seeking to discern the veiled features. We only laughed. When we reached the Rue de la Paix, we entered the jewelry shops. At sight of so many marvels, you can judge of her amazement; she thought herself in a dream; we spoke Turkish, and the puzzled shop-keepers regarded with surprise the strange beauty with her Asiatic grace, such as they had evidently encountered for the first time.   This all amused us, and it is needless to add that I left these tempting places with my purse very much depleted.

We have already made several of these excursions, and Kondjé-Gul is adorable in her child-like joy. Transported, as by magic, from the monotonous existence of El-Nouzha into the midst of splendors, of liberty, of life, she walks about as in a dream; the space and air intoxicate her. We make a thousand plans; in the very first place, we decided that she shall take up a definite line of action in respect to my wives and that she shall live separate in another part of the hôtel, where she shall have her own servants. We shall thus be able to see each other without restraint, and she will no longer have to submit to the disdain of the others, who take her apparent disgrace too seriously, since our arrival in Paris.   My proud Kondjé-Gul, conscious of her ascendency over me, would assuredly some day make an outbreak.   Besides, as I have already told you, she offers me a more and more interesting subject of study.   You must understand how captivating it is; here is a soul which I see born and which I am instructing.   Her wonderful intelligence surprises me over and over again.   I constantly discover an originality of views and sentiments in regard to the affairs of our society and our manner of living, the justness and aptness of which plunge me into astonishment; her progress is surprising, and knowing that she still lacks much of being *civilized*, as she says, she is eager to learn all.

My uncle and my aunt are in Paris.

CHAPTER XVII.

A month without news, you write me. And you speak ironically of my leisure, and you rally me upon that famous system which I boasted of as a simplification of life. If I judge from what you say, you believe me to be harassed with those very troubles and worries which I justly pretended to be free from; you imagine me going, coming, running about, incessantly occupied with my four wives, and never having any time to write you.

Once installed here, my four wives leave me much freer than the least of my former love affairs. No worry, no jealousy, no fear. It is not like a French entanglement which takes entire possession of you; forces you to follow the beloved object to the theatre, to conduct her to balls, to contemplate her coquetting with some intimate friend, who will perhaps be her lover to-morrow. My more modest love is hidden in the heart of my harem, and I am always expected. I have my key in my pocket. At any moment I can go there, without quitting my club, society, my work, or my pleasure an hour sooner. Such is that agitated existence which you suppose I am living.

However, as was to be foreseen, great changes have taken place within my household, where the Turkish element has, in part, disappeared to make way for the necessities of civilization. The transformation of my almehs is now accomplished. Hadidjé, Nazli, and Zouhra went the other night to the opera. I must confess, though, that their emotion was so strong at this first bold attempt that from my seat on the floor where I watched their arrival, I thought for a moment they were going to turn and run away. In their drives, and not without some coquetry perhaps, they had already, little by little, become accustomed to being seen; but, when they found themselves suddenly in the box with their faces uncovered to the gaze of a thousand infidels, all their resolution, all the courage amassed for this momentous occasion was put to flight. Odd as this strange senti- ment of Mussulman modesty may appear to us, they felt, they told me, almost an impression of nudity in showing themselves without veils.

However, the first emotion overcome, thanks chiefly to the exhortations of Mohammed, they succeeded suffi- ciently well in concealing their alarm, which might seem at a distance to be only a sort of excessive timidity. The rising of the curtain upon the first act of Don Giovanni happily turned their thoughts in another direction. During the *entr'acte*, their box soon attracted universal attention; the indolent grace of the Oriental type, although tempered by the Parisian costumes, could not fail to create a sensation. Who was that old man and his three peculiarly beautiful daughters? In the Jockey- Club box, where I went to listen to the remarks, conver- sation was as eager as after some great political event; Mohammed was in turn reported to be an American millionaire, a Russian prince, an opulent Indian rajah. From a certain smile that I designedly affected, they soon divined that I flattered myself with knowing more than anyone else; they surrounded me, they pressed me with questions; I had already made up my mind that it was better to set all uncertainty at rest in order to avoid too indiscreet inquiries being made. I revealed simply what was not far from the truth that

"Omer-Rachid-Effendi was a rich Turk whom I had had the honor of knowing at Damascus, and who had come to settle in Paris with his family." I insured myself thus against any suspicion of mystery, in case any accident should some day reveal my visits at the hôtel in the Rue de Monsieur.

Matters are therefore arranged, as you see, in a definite fashion. This new existence is one round of enchantments to my almehs, and I have truly at this moment an ideal harem, without the monotony which results fatally from the system of isolation. Under the influence of our refined customs, their ideas are, little by little, transformed. They have French maids, and the study of our worldly elegance reveals to them a thousand new forms of coquetry. My little animals have become women; this sentence alone tells you all the charm of this adventure, of which you alone in the world possess the secret.

As we resolved, Kondjé-Gul is separated from her too jealous companions. Hadidjé, Zouhra, and Nazli see in this action only the confirmation of her disgrace, and believing her banished to a corner of the hôtel, they think themselves more and more assured in their triumph. The discretion of my servants is beyond all praise; they serve like the mutes of a seraglio; the result is that we are free as air. When I wish to go out with *her*, I make a short visit to my wives; at the end of a quarter of an hour of chatting, I leave them and go to my carriage in which my favorite is hidden. You see how ingenious, simple, and delicate it is; but yet there is in this arrangement a sort of embarrassment for me, and for my poor Kondjé-Gul an isolation very hard to bear. She devours all the books I bring her; but the days are long, and Mohammed, monopolized by the others, can not accom-

8

pany her out. So I have thought of removing her entirely from the harem to free her from the disdain which the others still find, at times, occasion to inflict upon her. The difficulty was to procure a chaperon, a sort of sure and proper duenna, whom I could place with her in some separate house; this duenna is found. The other day we were talking of a little hôtel which I had found at the top of the Champs Elysées, and of an English governess who seemed to me to possess the necessary qualities.

"If you would like," she said, " all this could be much more easily arranged."

"How?"

"Instead of this governess, whom I don't know, I would rather have my mother. I should be so happy to see her again!"

"Your mother?" I cried in astonishment. "Do you know where she is then?"

"Why, yes; I write to her often."

She then told me the whole story of her life, which I had never dreamed of asking her about, believing her alone in the world, and it was quite a revelation of those Turkish customs which seem so strange to us. Kondjé-Gul's mother was a Circassian who came to Constantinople to enter the service of one of the sultan's *cadines*. Kondjé-Gul being very beautiful, even as a child, the ambitious mother had hoped for a brilliant career for her. To insure it to her, according to a custom common enough among Mussulmans, she had given her, at twelve years, to a family who was charged with bringing her up better than she, the mother, could have done it, until the day when she should be of age to be sought either as *cadine* or wife; the latter object was accomplished as you

know by means of quite a large sum offered by Mohammed. Poor Kondjé-Gul then followed him to her fate.
She told me, finally, that, some years since, her mother
had found a better situation for herself with a French
consul at Smyrna and had learned French.   Kondjé-
Gul's idea was a capital one and I adopted it; she wrote
at once to Smyrna, and some days after, she received an
answer.   I have sent the necessary money and in a
month her mother will arrive.   I have leased the house
in which they will live together; it is the little hôtel of
Comte de Téral, who is returning to Lisbon, and it is just
the thing we want.

CHAPTER XVIII.

You complain again of my silence, and you write to me
loading me with reproaches, mingled with sarcasm, which
does not hide your puerile curiosity.   In fact one would
say, from the tone of your letters, that I am ever subject
to strange occurrences, and that you hope every day to
hear of some catastrophe.   To-day your hope of an important event shall not be disappointed as I have a certain piece of news to announce to you.   The event is of
the most severe moral order, so you can listen to it without fear.

You know that my uncle and aunt have been in Paris
for the last two weeks, and they will remain here all
winter.   The hôtel in the Rue de Varennes has returned
to its former glory; receptions, dinners, in fact the round
of entertainments that you know, adorned this time with
the grace of the Countess de Monteclaro, which gives a
charm to our family life which was wanting heretofore.

My aunt has found a young cousin of her's here, Count Daniel Kiusko, a charming fellow with whom I have become very friendly; these details given you, I return to my story.

The other morning after breakfast, as I was going to my room, for, whatever you may think, I am working a great deal, my uncle detained me, and without more preparation, said:

" By the way, André, I expect to dinner to-day Madame Saulnier and Anna Campbell, your fiancée; I shall be glad to have you make her acquaintance. If, by chance, you are curious to see her, don't make any engagement at the club, and come home early."

" Indeed!" cried my aunt laughingly, and without giving me time to answer. " From your way of putting it, I should think it was a doll you were intending to give him for a birthday present."

" How under the sun do you think that, my dear?" asked the captain with his imperturbable coolness.

" I think that their becoming acquainted before marrying is an absolute necessity."

" Bah! they have at least a whole year before them. There is nothing romantic, beside, in the affair. Well," he continued, addressing me, "if you want to see her, you know you can."

" Exactly!" added my aunt. " Do you, André?"

" But," I replied, laughing at their discussion, " I think that my uncle has no more doubt than you of my eager desire to make the young lady's acquaintance."

" Then, it is all right!" said my aunt, gaily. "At seven o'clock precisely, my dear nephew, you will fall in love."

At this last touch of irony, my uncle did not move a muscle; he chose a cigar and remarked that they were too dry. My aunt took advantage of the occasion to continue her conversation with me.

"Between ourselves," she said, "you know that you have not much to complain of; she is charming, and you have made a great mistake in not seeing her sooner."

"I was waiting for my uncle to decide the matter."

"You ought at least to be obliged to him for letting you meet, *by chance*, before the wedding day," she continued.

"I suppose you think I meant to marry them blindfolded," said my uncle, at these words. "That is a good specimen of woman's exaggeration. Would you have liked me to present her to him, after my last voyage, a little girl of fourteen, thin, ungraceful, and ill-formed, as you all are at that age?"

"Thanks! say simply frights!" replied my aunt, with a courtesy.

But my uncle was in for a discourse, and he continued :

"Who would have left in his mind the unpleasant remembrance of a little flat, angular creature with arms like laths, and hands and feet as long as that."

"Poor little thing! You make me shudder. So, with rare prudence, you enveloped her in mystery."

"Pshaw!" exclaimed my uncle. "She is now a fine, strong, healthy girl who promises to be a suitable wife for André, and despite your ideas on that point, I maintain that I have done well in bringing them up apart from each other, in order to leave a freshness in their sentiments, and that there should not be that painful transformation of the heart, always disagreeable with two children who have contemplated each other eating tarts. They will see each other now as they must take each other for better or worse. The rest is their

own affair. If they love each other, they will make a
love match; if not, a marriage of convenience, which is
worth quite as much."

My uncle having thus concluded, I had nothing to do
except to declare my deference to his wishes. You will
easily understand that I impatiently awaited the moment
of this first interview, and that in the evening I was in
the *salon* long before the arrival of my fiancée. My
aunt was in ecstasies, as every woman is at the approach
of a romantic incident, and she did not fail to remark
my punctuality. As for the captain, he read his paper
tranquilly, like a mortal superior to the bagatelles of
sentiment; he was in the midst of a political discussion,
when a servant threw open the doors, and announced:
"Madame Saulnier and Mademoiselle Campbell."

I must acknowledge that I felt a slight excitement.
A lady of about forty entered, followed by a young person in conventual costume. I rose, while my uncle went
to his god-daughter and kissed her kindly on the forehead;
then, taking her by the hand, he led her to me, with a
dignified and ceremonious air, and said simply:

"Anna, this is André, your future husband! André,
this is Anna, your future wife!"

This form of introduction, precise and laconic, left no
room at least for doubt, and showed us at once our position.
I kissed my fiancée's hand, and then naturally had an opportunity to observe her. Anna Campbell is to-day seventeen, neither tall nor short, thin nor stout. She is neither
blonde nor brunette; she has a round chin, an oval face,
a medium nose, average forehead, average mouth, with
rather pretty blue eyes. She is pleasant looking rather
than pretty, and her features indicate great amiability
and perfect health. My uncle took care to point out to

me that her figure would probably be beautiful, although
her feet and hands are rather large. In short, my lot is
not a bad one, quite the contrary, and "all promises
well," as my uncle says.

The dinner was very gay. Anna Campbell, although
a little intimidated by my presence, showed no embarrassment. Nothing seemed strange to her, and everything in her manners and appearance revealed the perfect
ease of a child of the house, who had come to pass a
holiday there, and who felt as much at home as I did.
I perceived that she knew the hôtel as if she had been
brought up there, and I learned in fact that when I
was at college, she and her aunt had lived there for six
months. From all this, there resulted a certain graceful
familiarity with my uncle and aunt, totally unlooked-for
by me. Brought up separately and unknown to each
other, we met for the first time in the presence of him
whose common affection had bound us to each other
since childhood, and there was something pleasant in
the idea.

Once, during dinner, my uncle asked for the pickles.
" They are near André," said Anna.

The meal over, we left the dining-room. According
to a Russian custom which my aunt has introduced
among us, I kissed her hand and she kissed me on the forehead. Anna did the same; then, without even appearing
to think anything about it, she tendered me her cheek
and then kissed her god-father; after which she went to
the piano and played while we took our coffee.

" Well! What do you think of her?" my uncle asked
me.

" She is very sweet," I answered.

" Isn't she? She will make an excellent wife for you,"

he continued, stirring his coffee with the tranquillity of an easy conscience. "Go and talk to her; you won't find it hard work."

I went and sat down near Anna.

"Come and play the bass," she said, moving to make room for me, as if we had often played duets together.

The piece finished, we chatted of her convent, of her friends and the mother-superior, Sainte-Lucie, whom she adored, and all this with a confidence and familiarity which showed that she had spoken so often of me that she was accustomed to consider me as an absent brother. Of course, considering her youth, our betrothal is to remain a family secret, which will not be revealed until the proper time.

The evening passed away uneventfully. At ten o'clock, Anna left to return to the convent; when ready to go, she held out her hand to me.

" Good-by, André," she said.

" Good-by, Anna," I answered.

My uncle then carried me off to the club, and is now playing a game of whist.

While I am waiting for him, I must tell you an adventure which happened to him. You know that he is dead, since I have inherited his fortune. He will not come to life again; *the registry fees are paid*. From this odd situation result certain legal difficulties which embarrass him somewhat. Three months ago, at Férouzat, it became necessary for him to renew his shooting license, which was taken out seven years before; but as certificates of his death had been filed at the prefecture, they squarely refused to grant a license in the name of a dead man. He does without it, however, and shoots the same as ever! Moreover it happened the other

morning that he wished to draw from our bankers twenty thousand francs for pocket money. The cashier, who has known him for a long time, greatly astonished at seeing him alive, represented to him that it was absolutely impossible to open an account with him while he was dead and buried in the eyes of the law. My uncle, a sensible man, acknowledged the justice of this observation, and I had to intervene to arrange the matter. He thought no more about it and his determination is not shaken; but, straightforward, as in everything else, since that day, he has ordered to be engraved on his visiting cards, " The late Barbassou," and he never signs himself otherwise at our bankers; in this way, he pretends all is arranged in a right and proper manner.

" You see how simple it is," he says to me.

———

CHAPTER XIX.

My relations with Kondjé-Gul are becoming decidedly more and more attractive. The other day, I took her to Versailles, for the purpose of historical instruction for she is continuing the process of civilization. After we had visited the palace and the museum, we went into the park; she was thoroughly happy, rejoicing in the space, the air, the freedom from the harem, going into ecstasies at each step, questioning me about everything with a charming *naivete* that delighted me. At last we came to Diana's Bath, and found there a group of three very elegantly dressed young women, among whom I recognized, at the first glance, two former acquaintances of mine, well known in the light world. Young Lord B. was with them. They recognized me also; but with the tact of a perfect gentleman, Lord B., seeing me in such company, did not take any notice of me. No less discreet, as they usually are under such circumstances, the women did not bow; however, struck doubtless by the peculiar beauty of my companion, they could not help betraying so ardent a curiosity that Kondjé-Gul perceived it. Quite naturally, I passed them without a glance. We walked around the place, I explaining the mythological story, and then we went away.

"Who are those ladies?" she asked me, when we were a little distance off; "they know you, I am sure."

"Yes," I answered, with an air of indifference, "I have seen them once or twice."

"The young man who was with them looked at you as if he were one of your friends; why didn't you speak to him?"

"Because you were with me, and he, on his side, was escorting them."

"Ah! I understand," she said, "they are doubtless the women of his harem?"

"Precisely," I answered, with most admirable coolness, "and, as I have often told you, according to our customs, the harem is always—" As I sought vainly for a word to express my meaning, she burst into a silvery peal of laughter.

"What are you laughing at, you madcap?" I asked.

"I am laughing at the stories of your harems you still tell me, as you would that idiot of a Hadidjé. I let you tell them; what matters it to me, since I love you? I prefer the happiness of being your slave to the condition of those women whom you encounter without even deigning to notice them."

"What?" I cried in surprise, "you are already so wise, and you have hidden it from me?"

"After what you have given me to read, to form my mind according to your ideas, it was a foregone conclusion that I should some day discover the truth! But I was waiting to be very sure of my newly-acquired knowledge," she continued, smiling. "There are so many things in your country still, which I do not understand. Now you will explain them to me, won't you?" she added, cajolingly.

"Coquette! It seems to me that you have nothing to learn."

"Oh, yes; I know very well, in spite of everything, that I am to you only a curious plaything, an odd creature, something like a rare parrot that you are fond of, perhaps, for its pretty plumage."

"Ah! you know that last point at least!" I retorted, laughing.

"Yes, monsieur," she replied, in a tone of conscious pride. "I know that I am beautiful. Don't tease me," she added, with an adorable little grimace; "what I am about to say to you is very serious, for it comes from my heart. I was born for another life, for other sentiments than yours, and I know that I possess nothing of that which renders, it is said, the women of your country so attractive. They have a different turn of mind, different ideas from mine, which you call the superstitions of a young barbarian; all that I wish to forget in order to be able to understand you and to have no rivals."

"Are you very sure you would not lose by the change?"

"Thanks. That is meant for a compliment, I suppose."

" The fact is," I answered, " that what I love in you is that you resemble in no respect the women we have just met."

" Oh!" she cried, with an indescribable movement of pride. " It is not women like them I envy! But I see others whom I would like to resemble, in their manners and ways, I mean. If you were kind, do you know what you would do?"

" What?"

" It is an idea, a plan, that I dream of constantly. You won't laugh at me?"

" No; tell me of this wonderful project."

" Well, if you want to make me very happy, you will place me, for a few months, in one of those convents where your young girls are educated. You must come and see me every day, so that I shan't be too unhappy away from you."

" What an absurd idea!" I exclaimed, laughing. " A Mohammedan in a convent!"

I had great difficulty in making her understand how foolish her project was; but, while showing her the great obstacles such ambitious aspirations would have to encounter, I ended, myself, by gradually falling into her views. The attempt, indeed, would be most interesting. With Kondjé-Gul's character, it would be a psychological experiment interesting in the highest degree, and in her I found a marvelous subject. With her enthusiastic heart and ardent temperament, what would result from the sudden transition from the ideas of the harem to the subtle refinements of our world? I did not indeed conceal from myself that such an attempt was not without danger. But did not Kondjé-Gul already understand that the yoke in which my houris believed was only an imaginary one?   And would it not be better, in this case, to perfect the work of regeneration?

In short, I yielded to her entreaties, and when we returned to Paris, the great question was decided.   The next day I set to work to insure the execution of the plan, which was not, however, without its difficulties.

CHAPTER ˙XX.

After searching for a week, I discovered, in the Quartier Beaujou, an establishment for young girls, directed by a Madame Montier, an admirable person of perfect manners, whom reverses of fortune seemed to have prepared expressly to civilize my Kondjé-Gul.   The house never has more than three or four scholars; two young Americans are at present finishing their education there.   Nothing could be better suited for my purpose; I must confess, however, that at the moment of executing it, I felt a certain embarrassment.   I could certainly have presented Kondjé-Gul as a young foreigner, prematurely widowed and desirous of receiving a French education; but I soon saw that this would be a useless complication.   It appeared to me preferable to make her understand the necessity of extreme prudence.   So, one evening, when she returned to the great subject of her thoughts, I said to her :

"I have a great piece of news to tell you; I have found a charming school for you."

"Truly?   You consent to realize my dream?" she cried, embracing me.   "Oh! dear André, how good you are!"

"But, I must warn you.   This realization of your

dream is possible only at the price of sacrifices which, perhaps, will cost you a great deal."

"What sacrifices? Tell me quickly."

"In the first place, hard work, and then the sacrifice of your liberty; for, during all the time you pass at this pension, you can not go out."

"What matters that," she cried, "provided I see you every day?"

"It is precisely that which is impossible."

"Why?" she asked, ingenuously.

"Because, according to our customs, young men are not admitted to young ladies' boarding schools," I replied, laughing.

"But I belong to you," she exclaimed in astonishment; "they won't be surprised if you come; are you not my master?"

"That reason, a good one for you, would constitute exactly the obstacle, for no one must suspect that you are my wife. Mohammed alone will present you as a young lady confided to his care, and for reasons which you will understand later, all the time that you pass at your studies, we must be separated." I then revealed to her the truth in regard to our social customs. When she learned that our laws made her free and the equal of any French woman, and that I had no rights over her, she turned upon me a look of inexpressible anguish.

"What do you tell me?" she cried, throwing herself in my arms. "I am free, mistress of my life? I am not yours forever?"

"You are mine, because I love you," I said quickly, seeing her emotion, "and as long as you do not wish to leave me——"

"Leave you! What would become of me without you?" And her eyes filled with tears.

"Foolish girl that you are!" I said, touched by such real sorrow, "you exaggerate the consequences of my words; your liberty will change nothing in your life."

"Why did you tell me the cruel truth, then? I was so happy, believing myself bound to obey you and love you."

"It was necessary to do so, since you wish to learn our ideas and customs. Your ignorance was dangerous, your very questions might have made you betray a situation which must remain a mystery to all the world, and— in the pension especially, where you are going to have companions."

I could scarcely console her for the terrible thought that our laws did not allow slavery. But her desire for instruction remained strong and ardent. In short, two days later, Mademoiselle Kondjé-Gul entered Madame Montier's institution, presented by her guardian, the worthy Omer-Rachid-Effendi, who made all the arrangements with that majestic air he brings to bear upon everything.

Although I held myself carefully aloof, I watched over and directed everything none the less. Every evening Kondjé-Gul writes to her guardian, and her letters soon reach me. They tell a very curious story, I assure you. For a week, Kondjé-Gul, a little timid at first, surprised at all that surrounded her, seemed almost stunned. Not daring to open her lips, fearing to show herself too barbarous, she observed carefully, and her reflections on matters and things were most peculiar; then, little by little, I saw that she was becoming more brave. Gradually growing more accustomed to her new life, she soon

threw aside her reserve; the first degree of her emancipation is now passed. Her childish character, the oddness of this daughter of the Orient, have made for her the
strongest friendships, and nothing could be more charming than the stories she writes me of her enthusiasm for
her friends, Maud and Suzannah Montaigu, who are, in
her eyes, the dreamt-of perfection. The plan of her
studies, fixed by myself, is naturally of a limited description; music, history, and a superficial knowledge of literature. She will acquire there an insight into our ideas
and that feminine delicacy which only comes from contact with a woman of good birth. A few months'
sojourn at Madame Montier's will suffice for this worldly
initiation, and the cultivation of her mind can then be
finished by private masters.

In the Faubourg Saint-Germain, my harem retains its
Oriental charm; it is a page out of the Thousand and
One Nights, where I realize, in the heart of Paris, the
dreams of a vizier of Samarcand or Bagdad. There,
with closed shutters, the *salon* illuminated by lamps
which shed a soft light, while I watch the blue circles of
smoke from my nargileh float in the perfumed air, my
houris lull me to sleep with the music of taraboucks.
By the way, I must answer the sarcastic remarks in your
last letter.

I must declare, in the first place, that I have never
pretended to be a superior being, inaccessible to human
vanities, as you claim. I admit that, like anyone else,
" I feel the foolish satisfaction which every man experiences at seeing the success of the woman he loves."
The effect produced by my houris upon those whom you
call the genteel loafers of Paris, has suddenly given them
new charms in my eyes. The mystery which surrounds

them, the foolish conjectures I hear in regard to them,
all this, you say, excites me like a fool. You do not ask
me, I suppose, to defend myself, because I am subject to
that human weakness which leads us to appreciate our
felicity by reason of the envy which it provokes? What
is the use of analyzing my passion or casting my
love into the flame of the crucible to obtain its compo-
nent parts?

In the midst of my pagan luxury, you ask me if I
love. What is love? This question is an important one,
simple as it may seem; it touches upon that great problem of psychology which I have undertaken to solve:
"Which predominates in love, the heart or the senses,
and is to love four women at once, true love?" It is
evident that, in the restricted circle of our ideas, under
the yoke of our prejudices and our laws, we can only
conceive of a passion concentrated upon a single object.
Too far removed from primitive times and the patriarchal age, fashioned upon purer morals, we contemplate
only a recognized ideal. But, as moralists, as philosophers, we must acknowledge that there exists among the
Orientals another conception, another ideal of love, the
meaning of which we do not grasp. It is only by disengaging ourselves from the trammels and the rigorous
spirit of our social regulations that we can attain to the
comprehension of this lofty psychological problem. In
fact, what love is, no one has ever known. "Attraction
of hearts, interchange of minds." Those are only
words, suitable to the special case in regard to which
one wishes to employ them; the truth is that all our
definitions are full of inconsistencies. From the purely
sentimental point of view, we set forth this absolute
axiom: That the human heart can contain but one love

9

alone, and that one loves but once in a lifetime; now,
leaving out of the question the purely sensual part, love,
in its essence, is nothing else than a form of affection, an
expansion of the heart like friendship, like paternal or
filial affection, sentiments no less ardent, which we
recognize can be equally shared among many objects.
Whence arises this strange contradiction? Our ideas
upon this point come to us simply from our education,
from the influence of our manners and customs upon our
minds. On the shores of the Ganges, the Nile, or the
Hellespont, we should have quite different notions.
The most idealistic and impassioned Turkish or Persian
poet would understand nothing of our vain subtilties.
His law prescribing for him several wives, his duty is to
love them all, and his heart is equal to it. Will you say
this is a different love? By what right? What do you
know of it? Can you not understand, in this equal division
of tenderness, the charm which the feeling of their de-
pendence on him for protection has? Once more I
maintain our ideas on this point are always only a question of latitude or of climate.

My Kondjé-Gul's civilization forms the most delightful study for me. It is a whole romance full of grace,
and the ordeal which I have imposed upon myself adds
to it a certain charm. I must tell you that her sojourn
at Madame Montier's has led, little by little, to all sorts of
unexpected complications. Commodore Montaigu has
returned; the result is that the intimacy of Miss Maud
and Miss Suzannah with the ward of the worthy Omer-
Rachid-Effendi seeming to him perfectly proper, they
have become inseparable, and Kondjé-Gul is naturally
invited by her friends to certain little parties at their
father's house, which it would be impossible to refuse

without awakening suspicion. You understand, therefore, the reserve which has become more and more of a duty for me, as long as Kondjé-Gul remains at the pension. Our love is reduced to epistolary effusions, to furtive encounters, in which we employ all the ruses of separated lovers. There is a certain flavor in all this which enchants us, so true is it that being deprived of anything enhances its value. In the morning she takes riding lessons with Maud and Suzannah, whom their father accompanies to the Bois. I sometimes take a gallop out there to see them pass. She is charming on horseback, and the Montaigus are really very pretty, Maud especially.

. I forgot to tell you that Kondjé-Gul's mother, Murrah-Hanum, has arrived. She is a woman of forty-five, tall, quite distinguished looking, and still handsome. However, although she became Europeanized at the house of the French consul at Smyrna and even speaks our language exceedingly well, she still retains in her manners that oddness peculiar to the Circassian race or the women of Asia. Nonchalant and apathetic, you can read in her large, sombre, black eyes the morose resignation of fatalistic nations. When she met me, she overwhelmed me, in the Eastern manner, with the strongest marks of respect. I assured her of my desire to have her share all the luxury with which I intend to surround Kondjé-Gul. Her gratitude was calm and dignified, and she promised to show me the submission which she owes to her daughter's husband. In short, you can imagine the scene, the traditions of Islamism flourishing in full bloom.

CHAPTER XXI.

Quick! I must tell you of a new event, which gives a
most unexpected turn to my romance. By one of those
chances to which my life seems predestined, it happens
that the commodore is an intimate friend of my uncle,
and from this has resulted an encounter which has placed
me in the queerest position; you can judge of it yourself
without further preamble.

You have not forgotten, I think, Captain Picklock nor
the famous affair of the camels found by his help. The
captain is at present in Paris, having just returned from
Aden, and he has accepted the hospitality of the Baron de
Villeneuve, the former consul at Pondicherry, whom you
know. Two days ago we were invited to a farewell dinner given in his honor; there were half a dozen guests, all
of whom had been round the world many times and had
met each other in all sorts of places. The ladies were,
pleasant Baroness de Villeneuve, Madame Picklock, and
my aunt. You can imagine how old memories were recalled during dinner; after coffee, we went to the *salon*
where a whist table had been prepared, when my uncle
said these words:

"By the way, what has become of that good fellow,
Montaigu?"

"Montaigu?" answered the baron. "He is in Paris.
An invitation to the American Embassy prevented him
from dining with us; but he will be here this evening, and
you shall see him."

"Indeed!" said my uncle, "I shall be delighted to
meet him again."

Hearing this name I pricked up my ears. There was nothing to show, however, that the Montaigu in question was the commodore; I listened curiously. "Will he remain in Paris some time?" continued my uncle.

"All winter," answered the baroness. "He has come to see his daughters, whom he confided to my care, two years ago, on his departure for the North Pole."

"Oh! little Maud and Suzannah?"

"Yes; only, captain, little Maud and Suzannah are tall young ladies to-day," said the baroness, laughing.

There was no possibility of a doubt now, and I confess that I was troubled as I listened to these words. At the thought of meeting the commodore face to face, I determined to make my escape before his arrival. Although I was certain my secret was safe, and circumstances alone had brought about an intimacy I had not foreseen between Kondjé-Gul and his daughters, I knew I should feel embarrassed in his presence. Unfortunately, I was already seated at the whist table, playing dummy against Captain Picklock and my uncle. I played as fast as possible; but they threw down their cards with the most exasperating slowness, reproaching me meanwhile for my want of attention. Finally, I succeeded in losing the rubber, and rose, pleading a sudden headache, when, all at once, in the neighboring *salon* where the baroness was, a servant announced: "Commodore Montaigu."

Louis, imagine my consternation when I saw the commodore enter, followed by his two daughters and Kondjé-Gul, whom he presented to the baroness and my aunt as a school friend of Maud and Suzannah!

CHAPTER XXII.

You can imagine, I say, my consternation at this sight;
I felt myself blushing up to the ears. What was going
to happen? All retreat being cut off, I quickly hid myself behind a group of gentlemen who were conversing
together. A little timidly Kondjé-Gul received the
greeting of the baroness. I heard these words:

"I thank our friend, mademoiselle, for his kindness
in bringing you to us; Maud and Suzannah had spoken
of you so often that I was very anxious to know you."

The surprising beauty of the young stranger had made
a sensation, and with all looks fixed upon her, she
scarcely dared to raise her eyes. However, it was
necessary to ward off the danger which the least imprudence might lead to, and that, too, before the baroness should have the idea of presenting me to the commodore and his daughters. At last, by a rather skillful
maneuver, I succeeded in gliding behind my aunt.
Perceiving me, Kondjé-Gul could not repress a movement of surprise; but I had time to place my finger upon
my lips and by a rapid gesture make her understand
that she must not recognize me. Our meetings in the Bois
had fortunately prepared her for this necessary dissimulation, and she had enough self-command not to betray
our secret. My aunt turned at the same moment and
saw me behind her chair.

"Ah, André," she said, "come and let me present
you to mademoiselle."

Kondjé-Gul blushed as I bowed before her, and gave
me a graceful little courtesy. I was then introduced to

the commodore and his daughters. There being a vacant chair near them, the baroness made me sit down, and I soon became engaged in a general conversation. I must say that the liveliness of the Misses Montaigu rendered it much more easy than I hoped for. They had been brought up in the American fashion, and they had that freedom of manner which the rigor of a more narrow education ordinarily forbids to our young girls, under pretext of modesty. Kondjé-Gul, at first very reserved, little by little overcame her shyness, and I was astonished at the change wrought in her. Although it was certainly easy to see that she was a foreigner, her bearing, her gestures, and her words revealed a newly-acquired ease. Reassured by her behavior as to the danger resulting from our meeting, which I had at first feared, I gave myself up to the enjoyment of the occasion. As there were several young people present, the baroness determined to organize an impromptu dance, and commanded me to lead off with Miss Suzannah in a polka, which I willingly did.

"What do you think of my friend Kondjé-Gul?" she asked me, as we rested after a few turns.

"She is marvelously beautiful," I replied.

"You are of course going to ask her to dance with you?" she said, with a smile.

"I shall take care not to fail in that duty toward a friend of Miss Maud and you, mademoiselle."

"Miss Maud and I thank you, monsieur," she said, making a ceremonious courtesy; "but," she added, mischievously, "let me prepare you for a disappointment, which will doubtless be very painful to you: She does not dance!"

"What! never?"

"At the little parties at home we could never persuade her."

"She doubtless only knows Eastern dances."

"Undeceive yourself! She has taken lessons, like us, and she waltzes superbly; but she will never waltz even with the dancing-master. Maud or I are always her partners. She has principles about it, which, it appears, are absolute, and we have not been able yet to overcome them."

"If you will help me this evening," I said, "perhaps we shall succeed."

"A plot?"

"As a friend, acknowledge that it· is in her interest."

"I don't say the contrary," she answered, laughing. "But how can we bring it about?"

I could see poor Kondjé-Gul following us with her eyes and apparently envying us.

"Listen," I said, as if a sudden idea had come to me, "there is perhaps a means."

"What is it?"

"Let us take my aunt into our confidence; I can see them over there speaking Turkish. My aunt will perhaps have enough influence over your friend to convince her that she can, without sin, conform to our customs."

"Oh! yes," cried Miss Suzannah in delight. "Our plot is capital; how can we let your aunt know?"

"Does Mademoiselle Kondjé-Gul understand English?" I asked.

"No, not a word."

"Then it is very simple. After this polka, I will take you to your place; you tell my aunt in English of our plan, and ask her aid. I will come up, as if by chance, and ask for the next waltz."

This was aone. I watched from a distance the conference, all the details of which I could guess. While
Miss Suzannah was speaking to her in English, I saw
my clever aunt cast a laughing glance toward me. She
understood the request at once; she then turned toward
Kondjé-Gul, and with a careless air continued the
conversation. It seemed to me I could hear what
they were saying. I knew from the expression of
Kondjé-Gul's face the moment that my aunt broached
the subject, and the negative gesture with which she responded was so absolute, I was about to say so full of
horror, that, trembling lest she should close all retreat, I
thought it necessary to intervene as soon as possible.
So I advanced to the group, and, addressing the young
foreigner, said:

"I don't wish you to think me indifferent to the pleasure of dancing with you, mademoiselle. I intended to
ask you for the first waltz; but, alas, Miss Suzannah
assures me that you do not dance."

"You arrive to my rescue, André," said my aunt. "I
was just trying to convert mademoiselle to our customs,
by telling her that she would be taken for a little
savage."

At this word, which she had heard me repeat so often,
Kondjé-Gul cast a furtive, smiling glance at me. Miss
Suzannah joined my aunt in her entreaties, but the cause
was already gained. A waltz was commencing; Maud
took Kondjé-Gul's hand and placed it in mine; I wound
my arm around her waist and pressed her to me. During
the first few turns, Kondjé-Gul was very pale; I felt her
heart beat violently against my breast, and I confess I
was very near losing my coolness also. In a moment,
we found ourselves a little apart from the others; with

her head leaning on my shoulder, she murmured in my
ear:

"Do you love me still? Are you satisfied with me?"

"Yes," I answered quickly; "but take care, you are
too beautiful, and all eyes are fixed upon us."

"If they only knew!" she whispered, laughing.

I stopped a moment to allow her to take breath. Every
time anyone approached us, we seemed to be talking
those airy nothings one does at a ball, and when they
had passed, we spoke in a low voice.

"You naughty boy!" she said. "For three days I
have not seen you in the Bois."

"That was done through prudence," I answered. "I
will go to-morrow, and now I shall be able to speak to
you and your friends."

"You have a very pretty fan, mademoiselle," I added,
changing my tone for the benefit of Maud who came
toward us.

"Do you think so, monsieur," she answered. "Is it
Chinese or Japanese?"

But Maud had passed by.

"Listen," she said, "every time I raise my fan to my
lips, it will mean: I love you. What happiness it is to
dance with you! I can scarcely believe it is all real!
You will come and invite me again very soon, won't you?"

"You child! That can not be."

"Why?"

"Because it is not the custom, and it would be remarked."

"But I will not dance with anyone else," she said, with
a look almost of terror in her eyes. I had not thought
for a moment of this quite natural consequence of our
escapade, and I confess that the idea of her being invited

by anyone else struck me as one of those improbabilities which a mortal can not conceive.

"What is to be done?" she continued. "Oh! I beg of you, let me tell Suzannah that I must go."

"That would awaken suspicion," said I, no less troubled than she.

It was necessary at all cost to repair our imprudence. I imagined for her a sudden indisposition, a faintness which forced her to cease waltzing, and conducted her back to my aunt. This pretext would suffice to justify her refusal to dance for the rest of the evening.

I am perfectly well aware, my dear friend, that you will cry out at the recital of the odd feeling which struck me like a knife in the heart, at the idea of Kondjé-Gul dancing with anyone than me. But, what can I do? I am telling you simply a psychological fact and nothing more. Say, if you choose, that it is ridiculous and exaggerated, and that I am giving myself the airs of a crabbed sultan. The truth is, that in my harem, I have contracted habits of possession and susceptibilities which revolt at what I seemed indifferent to once. Contact with society will doubtless bring me back to that state of grace common to every honest husband. Perhaps, even, some day I shall proudly contemplate my wife, with bare shoulders, whirling about locked tightly in the arms of a hussar. But, just now, my disposition is less easy-going. I love as a master, and the thought that anyone would be allowed to press the tip of Kondjé-Gul's fingers fills me with a mad rage. That is what we are, we Orientals!

However, I brought Kondjé-Gul back to my aunt, and she danced no more. From a corner of the *salon*, I saw half a dozen of my friends go up to her, be presented, and with their hearts in their mouths, beg for the same favor which had been granted to me, and I laughed at their discomfiture.

The commodore, who, by the way, is a very pleasant, well-informed man, took a great fancy to me; he was so very kind that, in spite of my scruples, I was forced to accept his advances. His relations with my uncle would, beside, have rendered the cold reserve, which I had determined upon, suspicious. In short, by the middle of the evening, when he left with his daughters and Kondjé-Gul, whom he was to take back to Madame Montier's, I had, despite myself, made such an impression on him that he invited me to dine with him in conjunction with my aunt on the next day but one.

Although fate alone had brought about this complication, I must confess that, when I came to think it over, the consequences of it troubled me. Up to that time, by a compromise with my conscience which Kondjé-Gul's innocent character rendered almost excusable, I had been able to shut my eyes to the consequences of this boarding-school intimacy with two young Americans who were unknown to me. It might be only a passing acquaintance, after which all connection could be broken off. Miss Maud and Miss Suzannah would be ignorant of the secret situation which they could not suspect; but it was difficult for me to overlook the fact that intimacy with the commodore would singularly aggravate the whole matter. Certainly our society is a good screen for hidden romances; shadowy intrigues, ingenuous love affairs may be commenced and ended without any eye surprising them; but, certain as I was that nothing would happen to betray our astonishing secret, I was none the less troubled at the part I was called on to play in this family, of which my uncle was the friend. Face to face with the inexorable rigor of facts, it was difficult to be long deceived as to what the most elementary delicacy demanded of me. I had been able to observe, during this evening, that Kondjé-Gul had no longer any need of Madame Montier's instruction. The Hôtel de Téral was ready, and I had only to install her, therefore, with her mother, to establish at last in a definite manner the happy existence of which we had dreamed. It would then be easy to gradually draw away from the young Montaigus, and so all peril would be averted.

This decision taken, I wrote that very evening to Kondjé-Gul to prepare all for her return.

CHAPTER XXIII.

I had promised Kondjé-Gul to go the next day to the Bois, and my engagement had to be kept. The commodore, methodical in all things, had so arranged the morning rides that I knew that at nine o'clock they would be at the lake. At that hour the equestrian party turned the corner of the avenue. I went galloping along, pretending to try the different paces of my horse.

"Ah! there is Monsieur André de Peyrade!" cried the commodore.

I drew in my horse, as though greatly surprised at so agreeable a meeting, and saluted the young ladies.

"If you are not bound in any special direction," said Montaigu, "join us."

I turned my horse at once. The young ladies, who were somewhat excited by their exercise, were bent upon rapid riding, and their father strove in vain to confine

them to what he called a healthful trot. Finally, when
we came to a narrow by-road, it became necessary to
assume a more moderate pace. I took advantage of this
to place myself between Miss Suzannah and Kondjé-
Gul, and we talked of the previous evening, when they
had taken so early a departure. I naturally asked
Kondjé-Gul whether she had recovered from her
indisposition.

"Can you understand it," cried witty Miss Maud,
" when she waltzes so well?"

"You silly, I was only a little dizzy," answered
Kondjé-Gul "that was all. And if you had been in my
place, the same thing would have happened to you,"
she added with a smile at me.

"By the way, do you know, Monsieur de Peyrade, that
at the next ball, we can dance up to the cotillon,"
exclaimed Miss Suzannah with a radiant air. "We are
all going to leave the pension; Kondjé-Gul to-morrow
and we at the end of the week. We have just heard the
good news this morning; you can imagine how happy
we are. *Alhamdou Lellah! Chekrou Lellah!* as Kondjé-
Gul says, when she is pleased; that is Turkish. You,
who are so learned, do you understand that?"

"Yes, mademoiselle," I answered. "I believe those
words mean ' God be praised!' "

"Do you really know Turkish?" she cried.

"I know a few words."

"Oh! how lucky. Talk a little with Kondjé-Gul."

I did not have to be asked twice. Chance had afforded
us a most unlooked-for opportunity to talk together, but
out of prudence I only ventured upon an insignificant
sentence.

"Oh! you can say anything," said Kondjé-Gul, with a

smile. "They only understand three or four words that I have taught them."

"You received my letter, then?"

"Yes! and how happy I was! For I can tell you now how sad I have been away from you. Does my mother know?"

"Not yet. I shall go to see her on my way home and she will come to-day to Madame Montier's. Your house is a perfect jewel."

"I only hope you think me worthy of it," she said, with a sigh.

"Nonsense! You know very well I do."

"Truly? Am I enough *unturkeyfied?*"

"Certainly, since I don't think you need any more instruction."

"Between ourselves, now tell me frankly," she said, with an anxious look in her eyes, "do you think I have lost anything by it, my master?"

"On the contrary, your master finds you a thousand times more adorable."

"What! A thousand times only, and not one more? Oh! how cruel of you!" she cried, with such a mischievously reproachful look that we both burst out laughing.

I, of course, had to invent some story to explain to Miss Maud and Miss Suzannah our extraordinary gaiety. I escaped by saying that I had made a very queer blunder in the choice of my words. After this, our Turkish confabulation having lasted long enough, the conversation became general until we reached the entrance to the Champs-Elysées, where I took leave of them.

CHAPTER XXIV.

You know, my dear Louis, that whenever I take a notion into my head, be it wise or be it foolish, I follow it
out with the stubbornness of a mule.   This will explain,
perhaps, more than one of my follies.   In my opinion,
man, as the vindicator of personal liberty, is a will-power
served by physical attributes—a chance force created by
nature to dominate over matter.   Every man who gives
up or shrinks before an obstacle, deserts his mission; he
degenerates to the level of the beasts.   He becomes a
lost power, and disappears into space.   Such is my judgment.

This little exordium of lofty philosophy is necessary,
as you will see, to establish my principles before going
further, and to guard me against any rash accusation of
vacillation in my projects.   Science has its mysterious
pathways, in which men walk on tiptoe, without any
knowledge of where they will bring up.   The result is
that instead of the expected goal, new and vast horizons
are suddenly opened before them.   But my metaphor is
becoming unwieldy.

I merely mean to say that, having the honor to be my
uncle's nephew, nothing happens to me as to anyone
else, and that my designs regarding Kondjé-Gul have all
turned out contrary to my expectation and determination.

Kondjé-Gul and her mother are installed in the Hôtel
de Téral.   It would doubtless be superfluous to attempt
to depict to you the joy she felt at the termination of her

trial. The first days of her return passed like a dream of delight, and we were scarcely separated for a moment. Her metamorphosis this time was so complete that I seemed to be witnessing one of those fabulous *avatars* of India, and that another soul had come to inhabit this divinely beautiful body. I could never tire of watching her movements, of hearing her speak, and, in most exquisitely chosen language, express the same ideas and sentiments as my own. In this mind and heart, which I had formed, I discovered new emotions, a fresh love. And all these charms were mingled in a combination of youthful and entrancing graces which exhaled from her presence like the rare perfume of some Asiatic flower.

We have arranged the plan of our life. As she now thoroughly understands all our manners and customs, she appreciates the necessity of concealing, were it only on account of Maud and Suzannah, the secret of our happiness. Confiding in a bond which her religion teaches her to look upon as just and sacred, she knows that, for the sake of appearances, we must keep it hidden from everyone, as though it were a secret marriage. What would be the use, moreover, of tearing away the veil, and destroying the romance of so charming a love as ours, and reducing it to the commonplace of a vulgar intrigue? To treat her as a mistress—would not that be to ruin her?

When I sought to console her for the annoyance she must experience from such restraint:

"Do you wish to slander my heart?" she exclaimed, vehemently. "What care I for your country and its laws as long as I have your love? I want to hear nothing of your world, nor of its usages, nor of its conventionalities. I belong to you, I love you; that is all that

I see, all that I feel; I am neither your wife nor your
mistress. From the bottom of my heart I am far more
than either; I am your slave, and I am proud of my fet-
ters! Command me, make of me what you like; when
you no longer love me, kill me; that's all!"

"Agreed!" I cried, laughing at her excitement. "I
will have you sewn up in a sack and thrown some evening into the Bosphorus!"

A childish burst of merriment was her answer to my jest.

"Good heavens!" she said in confusion, "I have
already forgotten that I am civilized!"

The Hôtel de Téral is a gem, and seems to have been
expressly constructed for Kondjé-Gul and her mother.
On the ground floor, which is reached by a flight of
eight steps, is a *salon*, opening upon a kind of hall, something like an artist's studio, which is at once picture-gal-
lery, library, and music-room. Above the wainscoting are
white silk hangings with broad gray stripes, which contrast beautifully with the furniture, upholstered in rich
garnet velvet. About the room are scattered ancient
cabinets of carved ebony, covered with statuettes, vases,
books, and flowers. The whole effect is as luxurious
and coquettish as the abode of a young patrician who
restricts her circle to a small number of friends. Up one
flight are the private apartments, and above those the
servants' quarters. They have the number of domestics
necessary to a simple yet elegant household; three
horses in the stable, a pretty coupé from Binder's, and
nothing more. In short, the good taste which might be
looked for in a rich foreign family, composed of a
mother and daughter, mixing in society to a reserved extent, and desirous of avoiding attention.

The home life of Kondjé-Gul is well arranged to pre-

serve her from solitude or *ennui*. She is pursuing her
civilization with great ardor. Every morning from eight
to ten is devoted to study; governesses come from
Madame Montier's to continue their lessons; from one to
two is given up to singing and the piano. The curious
mixture of an ardent imagination and a newly-awakened
intelligence produces a wonderful effect upon the original
structure of her native beliefs and superstitions. I am
constantly surprised at her sage remarks upon the con-
tradictions, as they seem to her, of our social system.
After two o'clock the programme is: Dressing, riding,
walking, or paying calls with her friends, the Montaigus;
for, in spite of all my good resolutions, their intimacy has
steadily increased since they left the pension. As Kondjé-
Gul is continually under the ægis of her mother, which
is quite according to the conventionalities, it would have
been difficult, in fact, to find a suitable pretext for a
breaking off of the relations between them. Beside, I
reflected that, having been introduced by my uncle into
the family of the commodore, my meetings with Kondjé-
Gul at his house were devoid of any danger. It was
through Maud and Suzannah that I had been presented
to the beautiful foreigner, and no one could doubt but
that I had spoken to her for the first time at Madame
de Villeneuve's. If, therefore, some unforeseen contin-
gency should one day betray our secret, I was sure that
the commodore would not blame me, taking into consideration the circumstances.

You see nothing could be more correct so far as the
public is concerned. I know very well that you would
not fail to rigorously criticise my determination, if I
cared to listen to you. But, on my side, I contend that
respect for propriety consists principally in the respect

one has for one's self. Chance and her own charm have
created for Kondjé-Gul, in this foreign land, ties, which
possibly I should not have desired for her. For her
to be worthy of them, it is sufficient if we both pay
that tribute of secrecy to which the world has a right.
Society is too mixed, in my opinion, for you to have
dared to cry out "scandal!" if you had met Kondjé-Gul
the other evening with her mother and Commodore
Montaigu at the American minister's ball. The admiration which she excited would have disarmed you.

As might have been expected, the appearance of
Kondjé-Gul at a number of entertainments did not fail
to create a sensation. As she was the intimate friend of
the Montaigu's, she was soon taken with them to all the
balls to which the commodore escorted his daughters.
Two or three aristocratic houses like that of the Princess B.
and the Duchess d'A. have given her the *entrée* to all the
others. You know too well Parisian society not to be able
to imagine the exaggerated admiration which has greeted
the advent of this new star. I must say that the little
wretch perceives and enjoys it. The very mystery which
surrounds her enhances her attraction. Always under
the protection of her mother, who conducts herself with
great dignity, Kondjé-Gul has, moreover, something
about her which commands and receives respect. The
style of their house, their toilets, and a certain elegance,
only possessed by persons of distinction, are indisputable
tokens of wealth and rank. There is nothing wanting,
you must confess, to justify the success which her surprising beauty alone would have conquered for her. Moreover, the society reporters of the evening journals have
not failed to chronicle the appearance of such a brilliant
star. Only, by one of those errors, which are common

enough in their fraternity, they have declared her to be
a Georgian. As I have become decidedly intimate at
Commodore Montaigu's, I generally form part of their
group, without causing any suspicion, and my attentions
to her and to Suzannah have caused more than one pang
of jealousy, for, as you know, Kondjé-Gul does not dance.
This peculiarity, together with her mixture of sultana-
like fascination and simple girlish manners, has given
rise to the oddest conjectures. "Whence comes this
reserve?" "Is it modesty, timidity, or pride?" It is
known that she dances to perfection, for at certain
private gatherings she has been seen to waltz often
with Maud or Suzannah. There are whispers of some
unknown, jealous lover, whom she secretly adores. I
hear all these rumors and repeat them to her which
causes us much amusement. Sure of our secret, nothing
could be more delightful than the maneuvers we adopt
to blind all eyes. We have invented a language of signs
understood only by ourselves, the result of which has
been a number of scenes which were amusing enough.
The other evening at Madame de Y 's, she was seated
between Maud and Suzannah, and surrounded by
admirers. The young Duke de Marandal, one of the most
ardent among my declared rivals, was lavishing his most
captivating graces; Kondjé-Gul listened to him with a
delicious smile. Now I must tell you, that although
knowing that a young girl does not wear jewelry, with a
foolish idea, she has had a heavy gold bracelet riveted
upon her arm as a sign of her submission to me. And,
while the young duke was speaking, she glanced at me,
playing negligently with what she calls her "badge of
slavery!" You can imagine how we laughed over it
afterward.

Our little group has had an important and pleasant addition in the person of Edward Wolsey, a nephew of the commodore's, who would be a good match for Maud or Suzannah.

_____

CHAPTER XXV.

During the four months we have been in Paris, there has been nothing to mar our happiness, which no one suspects. Nothing could be more original and intoxicating than this love hidden from all eyes, and the delight of which you can imagine. Kondjé-Gul, charmed with her triumphs, is a universal enchantress; but my romance has become complicated by an incident which I must hasten to relate to you.

You will remember that my aunt met Kondjé-Gul one evening at the Baroness de Villeneuve's, and took a great fancy to her. A few evenings at the commodore's served to cement this friendship, the result of which was that she asked Madame Murrah and her daughter to dinner. My aunt loves young people, as you know; Suzannah, Maud, and Kondjé-Gul form such a delicious trio that she soon wished to have them at all her Thursdays. Kondjé-Gul has often met Anna Campbell, who leaves the convent twice a month. In short, our relations have become so firmly established that it would be imprudent to sever them; Kondjé-Gul, beside, is so happy and so proud of an intimacy which brings us so much together!

Among the frequent guests at my aunt's I have made mention of Count Daniel Kiusko, a fabulously rich young Russian, who owns platinum mines in the Caucasus Mountains and forests in Bessarabia. I have told you

that he is my aunt's cousin, which naturally forms a bond
between us. When he came to Paris for the first time, I
was delegated to introduce him. The task was an easy
one enough. He is tall and well-formed, a fine type of
the young boyar, with those decided traits characteristic
of a feudal lord. In less than a week, with the greatest
coolness, he lost half a million at *baccarat* at the club,
and all his other doings are in the same proportion.
You can understand what a standing such a début has
given him in society. A fortunate duel with a young
Brazilian showed him to be a crack shot and capped the
climax of his notoriety. His gratitude to me, and a certain admiration for superior abilities he thinks he has
discerned in me, have fostered our friendship; I have
become his confidant, his guide, and his mentor; in short,
I find in him a most agreeable companion, and, *arcades
ambo*, we scarcely pass a day without seeing each other.
He was at first a little surprised that I did not give myself up more freely to a life of pleasure, and suspected
that I was the victim of some mysterious passion, which
did not lower me in his opinion. With a pretense of
confidence, I revealed to him that I had a love-affair with
a young widow whose high rank obliged me to observe
the greatest caution. With perfect tact, he has never
alluded to it since! He is acquainted with the Montaigus,
whom he has met at my aunt's, and is generally regarded
as one of their suitors. Matters were in this condition
when the following incident occurred.

A few days since, I was in my aunt's boudoir; we were
chatting about one thing and another, she being engaged
upon some kind of needlework (her activity is wonderful), and I was playing with her dog, Music.

"By the way, André," she said, "I am charged with

an important mission, upon which I want to consult you."

"Well, aunt, my wisdom is at your disposal."

"Oh, be serious!" she answered. "You are about to undergo a formal examination, and I command you to answer me like an obedient nephew."

"You alarm me!"

"Don't interrupt me. This is to be a grave consultation."

"What! right away, without any preparation? Aren't you even going to change your toilet?"

"You impertinent boy! Does not this dress become me?" she cried.

"On the contrary, it is most charming."

"Well, then?"

"Pardon me! I was wrong to interrupt you."

"Very well. Let us continue. What was I saying?"

"That in that pretty dress of violet velvet, you were about to subject me to an interrogatory."

"Exactly. Attention and beware!"

"All right!"

"What do you think of Mademoiselle Kondjé-Gul Murrah?" she asked pointedly, with a steady look into my eyes.

This question was so unexpected that I felt myself blushing like a school-girl.

"Why," I answered, "I think that she is exquisitely beautiful."

"Exactly! Don't blush, my young friend," said my aunt, with a smile.

"I am not blushing."

"That is evident. Well, it is settled that you consider her exquisitely beautiful. So far, so good! Now, what

Kondje-Gul listened to him with a delicious smile.   Page 149.

are your relations with her? Tell me all, and conceal
nothing."

By this time, I had recovered my self-possession.

"Take care," I said, laughing in my turn. "Your
questions may get you into trouble."

"Don't be a goose! Don't try to put me off with a
jest, and let go of my dog's ear, which you are rumpling all
out of shape. There! that's right; always do as you are
bid. Now, answer me seriously, and with all the respect
with which a young girl like Mademoiselle Kondjé-Gul
Murrah ought to inspire you."

An odd whim seized me.

"I must tell you the whole truth?" I inquired. "You
desire it?"

"I demand the truth, pure and simple."

"Well, aunt," I said coolly, "you shall have it. You
are aware that Mademoiselle Kondjé-Gul is a Circassian.
Now, the fact is, she belongs to my harem. She was
purchased for me in Constantinople, eight months ago."

My aunt burst out laughing.

"There is no talking common-sense with such an
idiot!" she cried.

"You asked for the truth!" I retorted, laughing, in
turn, at the trick I had played.

"Do leave off your nonsense! Don't you understand,
overgrown child that you are, that if I speak of Kondjé-
Gul, it is because my eyes are open? It is perfectly plain
to me that there is some secret understanding between
you two. What is it? I can form no idea; but, innocent
as the matter may be, I think there is enough of danger
in it to warrant me in saying, 'Beware!' Mademoiselle
Murrah is not one of those society dolls with whom it is
safe to trifle and carry on a flirtation; he who loves her

once will love her forever, and remain enchanted, body
and soul."

"Why! She is Circe herself!" I cried. "This is
frightful!"

"Oh, you need not laugh!" she continued; "your fine
philosophical disdain will avail you nothing. An enchantress of such beauty is all the more dangerous, from the
very fact that she is just the kind of a girl to become the
victim of her own spells. In her heart smolder hidden
flames, which will one day burst forth and devour both
herself and the one she loves. That is why I am preach-
ing you this sermon, with the hope of restraining your
youthful imprudence from a flirtation which may entan-
gle you seriously, especially as you are already engaged
to another."

In spite of the light tone of *badinage* which my aunt
had assumed, it was easy to see that her concern for me
was real. I dropped my joking manner, and assured her
that neither my imagination nor my heart ran any risk
from Mademoiselle Murrah, and that "nothing could
possibly alter our present relations." This jesuitical
answer relieved her.

"In that case," she said, "I may make arrangements
for her marriage."

"Her marriage?" cried I, in surprise.

"Certainly. Did I not tell you at the outset of our
conversation that I was intrusted with an important
mission? My young cousin Kiusko is madly in love
with her, and has asked me to demand her hand from
Madame Murrah, whom I intend to call upon this very
day and broach the subject."

Although I had for a long time foreseen what would be
the consequences of a situation so totally opposed to all

social conventionalities, I must confess that my aunt's communication did not fail to cause me some trouble. The wonderful beauty of Kondjé-Gul had created too great a sensation for me to hope that I would be without numerous rivals. Her independent position, and her mother's reputed fortune, left the field open to aspirations and hopes which there was nothing to hinder from being announced openly. Nevertheless, well prepared as I was for such news, the announcement of Kiusko's pretensions affected me very keenly. There was no doubt but that his determination to marry Kondjé-Gul was the result of a deep-seated love, which opposition would only intensify. By nature energetic and cool-headed, endowed with a will of iron, and accustomed to see all things give way to his wishes, he had preserved a freedom of heart which was now to be abandoned to all the fervor of a first passion. But, in spite of my friendship for him, I could not disclose the peculiar circumstances by which he had been misled. To denounce Kondjé-Gul as my mistress, would be to banish her from the position she had gained in society; it would break her heart, and prove her ruin, without advantage either to Kiusko or myself. Beside, did I not owe her a greater loyalty than to my newly-made friend?

I determined, therefore, to preserve silence, and to await the progress of events. I knew too well that I could control them as I chose, to have any doubts as to the results. However, one apparently insignificant fact caused me some surprise. As I was informed of my aunt's projected visit, I went that evening to the Hôtel de Téral, expecting that Kondjé-Gul's mother would speak to me of it at once, but she said nothing. I naturally concluded that some obstacle had arisen, and the step had been postponed. The next day, without appearing to attach the least importance to my questions, I interrogated my aunt. She told me that she had called the day before upon Madame Murrah.

"Have you begun your overtures in this important matter of Kiusko's?" I inquired.

"Yes," she replied.

"And—did they consent?"

"Oh! you are in too great a hurry! Such things are not arranged so hastily among the Mussulmans. We went no farther than the preliminaries; I explained his wishes, and Kondjé-Gul must now be consulted."

"In the meanwhile, did the mother appear favorable to the proposition?"

"She would express no opinion at the first interview," said my aunt. "You know she has all the fatalistic composure of her race; however, when I made mention of Daniel's wealth, I thought that she was favorably impressed."

"Did she say what dowry she would give her daughter?"

"Dowry! Are you insane? We spoke Turkish; I treated the affair in the Turkish fashion, and I should have astonished her very much, I fancy, if, in demanding her daughter's hand, I had asked her how much she would pay Kiusko for taking it. That would have been contrary to all her notions. Are you ignorant that in the East, it is, on the contrary, the husband who pays a dowry to the parents when he takes away their daughter? And it strikes me as being a much more chivalrous and gallant custom, too. Beside, Kiusko does not care a fig for money; he loves her, and that is enough for him."

I was careful not to undeceive my aunt as to the hopes she had formed. Reassured by the way in which

Madame Murrah had played her part, I had nothing to do but to decide, according to circumstances, as to the form and time of a refusal.

As I was engaged in reflections of this nature, Count Kiusko entered, familiarly and unannounced; he shook hands with me with unusual warmth. From his happy demeanor, I guessed that my aunt had already communicated with him, and that he had lost no time in hastening to learn, in all its details, the result of her mission. As I had no desire to be in the way, I shortly pleaded the excuse of letters to write, and left them together.

CHAPTER XXVI.

We were to meet that evening at the Hôtel de Téral, where Maud and Suzannah were dining with Kondjé-Gul. Once or twice a week, either at Commodore Montaigu's or at Madame Murrah's, were given in the English style little entertainments, to which none but the most intimate friends were invited. Edward Wolsey, Kiusko, and myself were naturally three regular guests. In the course of this particular evening, Maud took it into her head to change the party into a masquerade for us six, and this proposition was unanimously adopted. Kondjé-Gul suggested that the three girls should assume Oriental costumes. This idea was hailed with enthusiasm, and they hastened away to put it into execution. The matter of disguise was not so easy for us male members of the party. We managed, however, to deck ourselves out with shawls, and some scarfs for turbans and sashes, and succeeded in presenting a respectable Turkish appearance. In about half an hour, the three girls made

their entrance in full odalisque attire. Veiled with thick
yashmaks, they advanced to Madame Murrah with great
ceremony, Maud, who was the shortest, walking first,
and Kondjé-Gul and Suzannah, of an equal height, bringing up the rear.

Wishing to keep up my character, I took Kondjé-Gul's
hand, and raising it to my lips, I addressed her in Turkish in terms of the greatest tenderness. A great burst
of laughter ensued, and the veil was withdrawn. I had
made a mistake; it was Suzannah!

"I have won my bet!" she cried, triumphantly.

I was ready to laugh myself at the trick; but as I
seized Kondjé-Gul's hand to repair my error, I found
she was trembling like a leaf. At the same instant, I
perceived that she was in a fainting condition, and she
almost fell into my arms. I led her to a sofa and lifted
her veil; she was pale as marble.

"Good heavens! What is the matter?" I exclaimed in
Turkish.

"Nothing, nothing," she murmured. "A sudden pain
in my heart, that's all."

"Child!" I said. "You must be mad!"

"Yes, I am mad and childish. I did not think you
could make such a mistake." Then, seeing that they
were all gathered round her, "It is all over," she added
in French, for the benefit of Maud and Suzannah, who
were greatly alarmed. "I have got out of the habit of
wearing Turkish slippers, and I turned my ankle." The
color returned to her cheeks, and she rose to dissipate
all anxiety. Her explanation was too plausible to admit
of any suspicion of the truth. The gaiety was resumed.
Maud and Suzannah were charming in their novel
sultana costumes. Maud sent me to the piano to play a

Turkish dance which Kondjé-Gul had taught them. I had an opportunity to observe Kiusko. Upon his strongly-marked countenance I saw such traces of emotion at Kondjé-Gul's accident that I asked myself if some sympathetic feeling had not acquainted him with its true nature, but I was soon reassured. Knowing, as I did, his passion, I read his countenance like an open book. He gazed upon Kondjé-Gul and seemed dazzled. Perfectly at ease in the Eastern garb which harmonized so well with her beauty, she had naturally such distracting allurements that the old leaven of vizier-like jealousy burned in my veins. Kiusko's bold glances were fixed upon her, and this caused me cruel suffering. I was consumed with bitter rage, until finally, after fifteen minutes of this torture, I could no longer contain myself, and drawing near Kondjé-Gul, I said in a low tone:

"Go and put on a *féridjié*."

She looked up in astonishment, and then, doubtless guessing my meaning, she smiled.

"Mother," she said in French, "ring for Fanny, please, I am a little chilly."

A moment afterward, she was wrapped from head to foot in the ugly mantle. I breathed freely again. Toward midnight, the commodore came for his daughters. As we were making preparations for departure, Kondjé-Gul moved a vase of flowers from a stand, and placed it upon the mantel-piece. This, in our secret language, meant that she expected me and begged me to return.

Ordinarily, I had my carriage in waiting to take me to the club, where I dismissed my coachman, and, after a few turns in the rooms, I would return to the Hôtel de Téral. This evening, Kiusko asked me to take him

along. From his manner, I anticipated an interview
from which I shrank.

"My dear fellow," said he, with a smile, as soon as we
were seated in my coupé, "I want to talk to you about
a very serious matter, so serious that it concerns my very
existence. You have encouraged me to regard you in
the light of a relative, and I should feel that I was doing
wrong to keep any secret from you. Unfortunately, I
know that my confession comes too late, and that your
aunt has anticipated me. The matter has reference to
Mademoiselle Murrah," he added.

"My aunt has indeed informed me that you com-
missioned her to make a proposal on your behalf," I
replied.

"And what do you say to it?" he asked, seeing that I
limited myself to a bare announcement of the fact without saying anything further. "Do you approve of my
resolution?"

"Really, my friend," I returned, laughing, "you have
taken me altogether too much by surprise for me to
answer so serious a question; beside, you know that in
matrimonial affairs, advice is never taken unless it agrees
with the preconceived notions of the recipient. One of
the best examples of consultations of this kind is Panurge's experience."

"That may suit your French disposition and turn of
mind," he remarked, "but for myself, who regard all
things something like a barbarian, the frank words of a
friend are far better than careful reserve. You have
known Mademoiselle Murrah longer than I, which has
placed you somewhat in her confidence. You are, therefore, able to assist me, or to warn me if you see any
serious obstacle which would make it best for me to

withdraw. You see it is no longer a question of a Panurge-like consultation, but of the true assistance of a friend."

My embarrassment was excessive; still he had luckily himself afforded me with a sufficient motive to remain circumspect.

"All that you say to me is very sensible," was my response, "but you must consider that any advice from me would be superfluous now, since your proposal has already been made, and by this time, doubtless, communicated to Mademoiselle Murrah."

"Aha! Do you think, then, that Mademoiselle Kondjé-Gul knew this evening of your aunt's message to her mother?"

"As to that, I can not say; but, as you have assumed that I am in her confidence, and granting that my opinion has some weight with her, is it not my duty, as a gentleman of honor, to only disclose such of her sentiments as I have her own authority to divulge, or, at the most, only those which have come to my knowledge otherwise than from herself personally?"

"I say, André," he answered, in a discouraged tone, "it strikes me, from your language, that you are shirking the point at issue. Your sage reasoning alarms me with the idea that there is some hidden obstacle which you do not dare to disclose, perhaps from fear of ruining certain hopes of mine, which you still preserve a wish to see fulfilled. Let me say for once and all that you are wrong. I tell you again, my whole life is bound up in this passion, dream, what you will, and that I am in love with Mademoiselle Murrah, be she rich or poor, or whatever may be her true position in society. So you may as well tell me everything," he concluded, laughingly, as though

11

he would protest against the possibility of any suspicion to her disfavor. "And you must see the futility of any recourse to subterfuge."

"Oh!" I exclaimed, "you are indulging in ridiculous fancies, and you thoroughly misunderstand me, if you attribute my silence to any discovery of impropriety on the part of the young lady. The idea of Mademoiselle Murrah being an adventuress strikes me as sheer madness."

"Then, on principle," returned he, tenaciously, "you do not disapprove of my design?"

"On principle, my dear fellow," was my laughing rejoinder, "I only come round again to the illustration of Panurge. Beside, your advances have already been made known to Mademoiselle Murrah, which vastly depreciates the worth of my advice, or at best can only give it, at this late stage of the proceedings, a very exceptional kind of value."

"You are right," he answered, evidently assured by my gaiety. "I have all of a lover's preposterous notions. I can conceive that you would not wish to undertake so serious a responsibility. Only," he added, "between ourselves, I went there this evening with the hope of arriving at some inkling of my fate. Now, there is one thing you can tell me without compromising yourself."

"What is that?"

"Mademoiselle Murrah is, no doubt, already aware of the proposal your aunt so kindly undertook to communicate. You had a short conversation with her; did she mention the matter?"

"She did not say one word about it, I assure you."

We had now reached the club, and our conference was interrupted by some acquaintances, who made their appearance at the same time as ourselves. The foregoing conversation had caused me a certain unpleasant irritation, which I was unable to throw off. I was ashamed of the false part I had been compelled to play, and, at the same time, the idea of his looking upon Kondjé-Gul as accessible to his vows made me undeniably angry. All at once, the thought came into my head that two days had already elapsed since my aunt had made her first advances, and I was astonished that Madame Murrah had not as yet spoken to me about it. I began to wonder whether Kondjé-Gul was really ignorant that Daniel loved her, and whether there was not some mystery about the affair.

In order to calm my fears, after showing myself in the parlors of the club, I returned hurriedly to the Hôtel de Téral, by way of the Champs-Elysées. Everyone there had already retired, except Kondjé-Gul, who was awaiting me, still attired in her fascinating odalisque costume. When she saw me, she threw her arms around my neck.

" Oh! you dear, dear jealous boy!" she cried, gaily.

" Jealous! Who? I?" I retorted, affecting not to understand, and thinking she was about to reveal her offer from Kiusko. " Why, please, should I be jealous?"

" Ah! now!" she said. " And I thought so, because you made me put on my *féridjé.*"

" Oh! is that it?" said I, as I saw she was still in the dark.

" Why, of course," she returned, making up a wry little face of displeasure. " I'thought you found me so pretty that you did not want the count and Edward Wolsey to see me in the costume which had been reserved expressly for your own eyes. But, I see, it was only because you feared I might take cold.   What a shock to my pride!"

"What a child you are!"

"Confess now!" she continued, with a bewitching little smile. "You *were* jealous."

"Well, yes, I confess," I answered, overcome, in spite of myself, by her grace. "I was furious at seeing you play the coquette!"

"Really?" she exclaimed, joyously. "And you won't love Suzannah?"

"Suzannah!   For heaven's sake!"

"But that is just where all the trouble lies. Just fancy, after we were all dressed, that silly Maud proposed that we should all make our entrance closely veiled, with the idea of confusing you all between Suzannah and myself. We adopted her project.   I was quite sure that you would recognize me, and that the count and Mr. Wolsey would be the only ones to make any mistake.   I jokingly suggested that we should accept whatever happened as an omen, and that the man who mistook Suzannah for me would be her husband."

"This was the cause, then, of your emotion, which I could not explain?"

"After what I had said, it was enough to frighten me. So you can imagine how happy I was, when I saw you jealous."

It was quite evident that I had been giving myself up to suspicion without due cause, and that Kondjé-Gul knew nothing. On reflection, I felt that I could only approve her mother's course in concealing a futile offer, which she undoubtedly, in her apathetic manner, considered of such minor importance that she did not judge it necessary to inform me of it on the very day the

proposal had been made. It was a matter to be arranged
between herself and me, and I determined to give her an
opportunity for the interview the next day.

Hardly was I up the next morning, when Kiusko
appeared, booted and spurred; we had arranged the
previous evening to ride in the Bois. As it was his usual
custom to go to the place of meeting alone, I guessed
that, on this particular day, he wished to give the impression, either through timidity or embarrassment, that
he was riding under my leadership, when we should meet
Kondjé-Gul. Resolved to avoid any new confidences, I
detained my valet and dressed myself very slowly, without pity for his impatience, but with the design of making
us late, a fact which compelled us, when once in the saddle, to make our way to the Bois at full gallop, a gait
little suited to conversation.

We did not catch up with the party until we reached
the Avenue des Acacias, a place which was the turning
point of the ride. I did not fail to observe Kiusko when
he saluted Kondjé-Gul. He blushed and stammered
out a general compliment to the young ladies. Kondjé-
Gul's face betrayed no emotion beyond the excitement of
the ride. We separated into two groups. Kiusko remained behind with Suzannah and the commodore;
Edward Wolsey and myself took the lead with Kondjé-
Gul and Maud, who were at swords' points as to
whether we should ride straight ahead or down a certain
by-road. Kondjé-Gul settled the dispute by turning her
horse abruptly into the latter.

"Who loves me, follows me!" she cried, laughingly.

I followed, and we found ourselves side by side.

"Great news!" she said to me, when Maud and Edward, who were behind us, were out of hearing.

"What is it?" I asked.

"Well, just imagine! Day before yesterday your aunt called on my mother when I was out, and in the most formal manner asked for my hand in marriage in behalf of the noble Count Daniel Kiusko. My mother told me of this early this morning."

"And what was your answer?"

"In the first place, I laughed; and then I told mamma to let you know of it at once, so that you might decide in what manner to repulse the enemy."

"That is simple enough," I replied. "She has merely to inform my aunt, when she comes again, that she has laid the matter before you."

"Will that be all?"

"Certainly," I said, somewhat provoked at the notion of her knowing of Daniel's love; "your wishes alone can decide it."

"My wishes? André, do you no longer love me?"

"Why do you ask that?" was my response.

"One would say that you wanted to recall that terrible freedom which frightens me so."

I saw that I had been stupid and brutal, and hastened to apologize.

"You were cruel!" she said, pointing to the golden fetter riveted on her arm.

We decided that I should go to her mother, and dictate the precise terms of a refusal which should leave no room for hope. At this moment we emerged from the narrow bridle-path, and were joined by Maud and Edward. Our ride was finished without any other eventful occurrence, unless it may be noted that Daniel watched Kondjé-Gul and myself very closely, as if he would have liked to have known what had been the subject of our

tête-à-tête. Resolved to put an end to all this embarrassment at once, I determined to finish up the affair that
very day.

Toward three o'clock, I went to the Hôtel de Téral,
and, in an interview with Kondjé-Gul's mother, I stated
precisely the terms of her response to my aunt, which
was limited to this formula, customary in such cases:
" Mademoiselle Kondjé-Gul Murrah is very much flattered at the honor Count Daniel Kiusko has paid her, but
regrets that she is unable to accept his offer." And, in
order to show that this was not one of those composi-
tions which are not to be regarded as final, I added:
" She will state, in confidence, that her heart is no longer
free, and that she is engaged to one of her relatives."
This semi-confidential answer had the merit of frankness,
after which no gentleman could press his suit without
offense. Kondjé-Gul was thus fixed in a position which
protected her from all importunate solicitation on the
part of my rivals.

———

CHAPTER XXVII.

You return again, my dear Louis, to your bragging
vein, and you air your wit at my expense. My Oriental
system falls to pieces, you say, at contact with the real
world, and with those sentiments which I pretended to
class among the prejudices of an effete civilization. You
do not perceive, crafty mocker, that there is not one of
your arguments which does not turn against yourself
and proclaim the superiority of harem customs. Is it
not evident that my mishaps, my troubles, my fits of
jealousy, which you designedly exaggerate, are caused
solely by Kondjé-Gul's emancipation, and that nothing

of all this would have happened, if I had not derogated from Turkish usages? Contemplate, on the one hand, the serenity of my relations with Zouhra, Nazli, and Hadidjé, that quiet, poetic, or sultanic existence, free from all annoying rivalry; and, on the other, see the difficulties and worries at once produced by our social system. Indeed, I don't know why I should trouble myself to discuss the matter with you.

Relieved by the assurance that Kondjé-Gul would be delivered from Count Kiusko's pursuit, after the declaration made by Madame Murrah to my aunt the next day, my mind was at ease again. I did not doubt the effect that such a categorical answer would produce upon Daniel. I knew too well how deeply he was in love not to foresee that the blow would be a heavy one.

I therefore expected to see him go away and hide his disappointment in some solitary retreat. To see Kondjé-Gul again after such a decisive rejection, would cause him suffering and revive his regret. It would, moreover, place both him and her in an embarrassing situation, to meet after his declared love for her. But, on the contrary, I was totally surprised to see him appear among us the next day, as calm as on the previous evening, and as if no annoying incident had happened. Day followed day, and there was no change. He seemed perfectly at his ease, and, as if confident of the final issue of his suit, he was only awaiting the hour which would crown his hopes with success.

This singular result of an absolute rejection troubled me not a little; but, somewhat embarrassed by the part I was playing in the affair, I had too squarely avoided my rival's confidence to say a word to him now. I began to suspect that Kondjé-Gul's mother had not fully

We found ourselves side by side. Page 165

carried out my instructions. I resolved to discreetly question my aunt on this point.

"By the way, my dear aunt," I said to her one morning, in the most indifferent tone I could assume, "you have not said anything more to me about Kiusko's marriage."

"Oh! that is all at an end," she replied. "He was too late; the heart of the beautiful Kondjé-Gul is already given away. She is engaged to one of her relations."

"He seems to take his discomfiture very lightly."

"Oh! don't be too sure of that!" she replied. "Daniel is not one of those weeping lovers who pour forth their complaints to the moon; he loves her, I saw that by his sudden pallor when I told him of her very clear rejection of his suit; but he has a will of iron, and you can be certain that if he is so calm it is because he still has some hope. For my part I shall not believe in Kondjé-Gul's marriage with her relative, until after they have left the church." Although it mattered nothing to me that Kiusko was still deceived by a remnant of hope, nevertheless, I felt a certain chill at such presumptuous insistance. He had officially declared his love and Kondjé-Gul could no longer feign to ignore it. There was something almost insulting to her in his easy manner which seemed to take no account of an engagement which she had made known to him, as a reason for her refusal. Reserved as he was, and although never a word betrayed his secret feelings, which he carefully veiled in our everyday relations, it was impossible not to feel the constraint of a situation, which, on his side, he appeared to think nothing of. This insolent confidence finally aggravated me to the last point of endurance; but one circumstance, apparently insignificant, soon turned my suspicions in another direction.

One morning, about ten o'clock, I accompanied my aunt on a round of visits to the poor. As our carriage happened to pass the Hôtel de Téral, I saw Daniel coming out. What was his business there? It was the hour when Kondjé-Gul was busy with her lessons, and certainly no time for calling. Such a discovery caused me so much anxiety that I had difficulty in concealing it. However, I reflected that Maud or Suzannah had perhaps charged him with some message, to take a book to Kondjé-Gul or something of that sort. Still, I wanted to have my mind set at rest. In the middle of the Champs-Elysées I made an excuse that I had an order to give to a carriage-maker, and leaving my aunt to return home alone, I went to the Hôtel de Téral.

As I had foreseen, Kondjé-Gul was occupied with her piano teacher. I sent up my card and was at once admitted.

"What! is it you?" she said, feigning, for the teacher's benefit, surprise at so early a call. "Have you come to play a duet with me?"

"No," I answered, "I was passing by, and I stopped to inquire if you had arranged anything for to-day with your friends the Montaigus."

"No; they expect me at three o'clock, that's all."

"You have not heard from them this morning?"

"No. Has anything happened?" she added in Turkish.

"Absolutely nothing," I replied, smiling. "My aunt brought me near here, and I wanted to say good-morning to you."

"How good and kind you are!"

She had not left the piano, and I had remained standing in order to show that I had only dropped in for a moment, as I was passing by. I shook hands with her, declaring that I did not wish to interrupt her lesson, and took my leave.

It was evident that Kondjé-Gul knew nothing of Daniel having been there. As I went out, I spoke to Fanny and gave her some instructions in regard to some flowers I was going to send. The girl was entirely devoted to me and her discretion was beyond question. But, not wishing to appear to question her in regard to her mistress, I asked her carelessly if the count had brought anything for me.

" I don't know, monsieur," she answered. " The count came here an hour ago, but he asked for mademoiselle's mother, who was expecting him, I think, and who gave orders to have him shown into the little *salon*, where she went to receive him. When he went out, he said nothing to me."

" Did he say anything to Pierre?"

" Pierre was not here, monsieur," replied Fanny. " The count spoke only to Madame Murrah."

" Ah! Very well!" I said, negligently.

My inquiries had ended in a curious discovery. What was the meaning of this interview of Daniel's with Kondjé-Gul's mother? I determined to penetrate the mystery, and went up deliberately to Madame Murrah's apartments. She did not appear surprised, whence I concluded that she knew I was in the hôtel and was prepared to receive me. On my side, I pretended to have come to regulate certain details of the household, for I always was obliged to help her in all things. She listened with that servile smile she always wears in my presence. When her attention was occupied with figures and estimates, I suddenly said to her:

"By the way, what did Count Kiusko come here for this morning?"

I thought the color came into her face, but I was not quite sure.

"The count?" she answered, in a tone of the most profound surprise. "I did not see him. Was he here?"

"Fanny let him in," I replied, "and you spoke to him."

Oh! yes; *this morning*, "she cried quickly, emphasizing the words. "Ah! my poor head! I understood you to say *last evening*. I understand French so poorly. Yes, yes; he was here. The poor young man is mad. This is the second time he has come to beg for Kondjé-Gul's hand. He is mad! He is mad!"

"Ah! he has been here before! Why did you not inform mé of it?"

"That is true! I had forgotten it," she replied.

I judged it useless to say more. Had Madame Murrah tried to conceal from me these visits of Kiusko? Or was not the very fact of her not having told me a proof, on the contrary, of the little importance she attached to them? To show her I suspected her, would, in any case, put her on her guard. Without alluding to the matter again, I continued my directions, as if I saw in the morning's incident only the puerile obstinacy of an infatuated lover. A quarter of an hour later, I took leave of her as cordially as possible.

Once out of the house, I calmly reflected upon the affair. Had I by accident surprised some understanding between them, or had my jealous mind taken alarm at some foolish interview which Kondjé-Gul's mother had not been able to avoid? Accustomed to a sort of passive submission, had she allowed herself to be intimi-

dated by a man who spoke to her in a lordly way?
Embarrassed with the part she had to play, had she
awkwardly let some imprudent word escape her? Would
not this supposition explain Daniel's singular behavior?
At all events, I made up my mind to watch my rival,
when an unexpected incident suddenly brought about
new complications.

One evening, as I arrived at the Hôtel de Téral, I
thought I saw a man hidden in the shadow of the next
house, and who appeared to be awaiting or watching someone. I always took prudent precautions, most often
superfluous, in this deserted quarter, and I never risked
entering by the secret door without first making sure
that no one was near. Puzzled by the motionless attitude of this man, whom it was impossible to take for a
casual passer-by, I went on and turned the corner of the
street without stopping, supposing that he would follow
me if he had come there to spy upon me. After I had
gone a few steps, I looked over my shoulder, but saw no
one. I returned; the man had not stirred. Impatient,
this time, I went straight up to him.

"What are you doing there?" I demanded.

"Ah! Monsieur de Peyrade!" he cried. "What! Is
it you?"

Surprised at hearing my name, I tried to recognize
the voice, which did not seem unfamiliar to me.

"Oh! you must have forgotten me," he said; "but it
is not the same with me, for you once rendered
me a great service. I will aid your memory: Antonin
Giraud."

This name recalled to me quite an original fellow
whom I had once sat beside in the lecture-room, and of
whom I remembered scarcely anything except the aston-

ishing facility with which he squandered his money with
true Bohemian carelessness. As I was little desirous of
renewing my acquaintance with him at that moment, I
cut short his effusiveness.

"Well! Monsieur Antonin Giraud," I said, "I repeat
my question: What are you doing here?"

"By Jove, monsieur, I don't know in the least! But
I think that, in my turn, I am going to render you a
service."

"Me, a service!" I answered, haughtily.

"Monsieur de Peyrade," he said, not in the least disconcerted, "there comes in the life of poor devils, who
struggle with all their might against ill fortune, a moment
when ruin seems imminent. Some years ago, without
knowing it, you saved me at such a moment. Will you
allow me to call on you to-morrow morning? I think I
shall be able to repay you!"

"What do you mean?" I asked.

"This place is not a good one for a conversation.
Beside, I repeat to you that I am absolutely ignorant
why I am here. In a few hours I shall know; let it '
suffice for me to tell you now that someone has an interest in watching that little door yonder. You can tell me
to-morrow what you wish to be known. May I ask you
at what hour you will do me the honor to receive me?"

"Come at ten o'clock," I answered, and I gave him
my address.

In trying to recall what the service could be that I had
rendered this fellow, I remembered that in my college
days, I had often lent him little sums of money at one
time or another. He was of a most curious type, a
mixture of the rarest gifts and an utter recklessness. A
former pupil at the École des Chartes, an indefatigable

worker or excessively lazy, as the mood took him, he possessed a wonderful amount of knowledge. Now a tutor of literature, now a professor of science, he lived from day to day, expending more energy in obtaining a dinner than he would have had to display if he had stuck to his work.

At ten o'clock the next day, my valet announced him. When he appeared, I was struck with surprise; the previous evening he had presented that shabby appearance he always used to. He entered now dressed in entirely new clothes, in which he appeared to take a puerile delight. I should hardly have recognized him.

"Monsieur de Peyrade," he said, sitting down in the chair I pointed out to him, "I have made a discovery. I was not wrong in promising you last evening interesting revelations, and I come with plenty of them."

"I am listening to you," I answered in a reserved tone, which doubtless showed him that I had not much confidence in him.

"Very well!" he said. "There is no need of a preamble. Let us go at once to the heart of the matter, for I see that I must prove to you that I am dealing frankly with you. After all, you surprised me last night in an occupation which it is impossible to be very proud of."

"I will defer my answer to that," I said, "until you have informed me of the object of your visit."

These cold words, and the tone in which they were uttered, arrested Antonin Giraud's attention. He looked at me, and guessing doubtless from my manner the effect he had produced upon me, he blushed scarlet.

"Indeed," he said, turning away his eyes, "I have every reason to believe that I have something to tell you of great interest to you, and in that case——"

"You have come to propose that I shall buy your revelations," I replied, completing his sentence.

He hesitated a moment, and passed his handkerchief over his face.

"Well! yes," he said, at last. "It may be worth your while."

"Then speak; I am listening to you."

I saw him make an effort to recover his assurance; but as he raised his head, as if decided to show effrontery, his eyes suddenly met mine.

"Ah! I am playing a miserable part!" he exclaimed, "and you must take me for a wretch!"

I saw no reason for answering, and my silence increased his trouble.

"See here, Monsieur de Peyrade," he continued, "I implore you, do not judge me by what I have just said. Last night, I swear to you, when I saw you again, I thought only of the kindness you had once shown me. Chance alone had led me into that wretched matter whose true purpose I did not know. I was offered twenty francs to pass the night there, and was told that it was to play a joke upon a friend. When I saw that you were the man in question, without even thinking of what your opinion would be of me, I had no other idea than to serve you, by revealing to you that I was charged with watching that house. I thought that, perhaps, you were in danger and that you must be warned. Then I asked for your address, to come and tell you all the details of which I was ignorant then, but which I knew I I could procure this morning. There! That is the truth!"

"Then, what is it you have come to tell me, my dear Giraud?" I said, changing my tone at the sincere confusion of the poor fellow.

"It is quite a story," he continued. "And you shall see that if Dame Poverty, my cross-grained spouse, has made me commit more than one folly, she at least gave me good counsel this time. Do you remember Zarewski, called the Pole, because he was a Prussian?"

"Vaguely."

"Well, your forgetfulness has not prevented him from making his way in the world. He has become a diplomate; some people pretend, however, that he only serves in the police force of a great foreign minister. Well, he appears from time to time on the Boulevard Saint-Michel. Yesterday, he met me in a café, and made me the offer I spoke of. He was in love with a duchess whom he suspected of infidelity, and he asked me as a friend to play the Argus last night. You know how well I fulfilled the mission as soon as you appeared. Well, I went to see the Pole this morning. I first gave him a report, telling him that nothing had occurred during the night. He laughed in my face, and told me flatly that I had seen you, that I had had a conversation with you, and that I had left the place when you entered the house. I saw I was caught, but to my great astonishment he gave me my louis all the same. He then questioned me about you, and said that, since I knew you, we had a great chance for a speculation, as you had doubtless very great interest in purchasing a certain secret. Hearing this, I saw that I must know what he meant; I hesitated just enough to excite him, and I feigned to fear that he was mixing me up in some political plot. He ended by telling me all. One of his friends is on the point of marrying a young foreigner, whom he adores; he has heard certain gossip about her. He does not believe it, but he wishes to be sure, because he suspects he has rivals.

12

I hesitated still, pretending not to be convinced by his story. He then gave me the names. The jealous love, is Count Kiusko, the lady, a young girl called Mademoiselle Murrah; the suspected rivals `are the Duke de Marandal and yourself. Once possessed of all the information I wished, I told him squarely that I had no taste for blackmailing. I added that you had once done me a kindness, and that I should at once warn you that you were watched. He then declared that it was too late to do that, as all they care to know is known now, and if you did not prevent it by paying up this very morning, the information would be given to Count Kiusko. He showed that after all I should be acting in your interest. That you were a nabob, able to offer us a large sum. He gave me these clothes to come and see you. You see how fine I am, but that did not prevent you from taking me for a rascal."

"Well, Giraud," I said, touched by the poor fellow's evident remorse, "give me your hand, which you forgot to do when you came in."

He looked at me in astonishment.

" But," he said, hesitatingly, "I don't know that I dare to now."

"Pshaw! throw aside your friend Zarewski and the adventure of last night, which is of no importance to me, and tell me how, being what you are, you have so wasted your life."

"What! Wasted!" he gasped. "Why, since I saw you last, I have worked like a negro, and learned six languages. I know Sanskrit to-day as well as Burnouf. Wasted! But there is no question of that," he continued, interrupting himself. "And there is question of you. You don't know the whole story yet. You are surrounded by a perfect network of spies, and if there is anything you don't care to have discovered, beware!"

He then told me that for ten days both myself and the Duke de Marandal had been subjected to a system of constant espionage. Our slightest movements were watched, as well as those of Kondjé-Gul, and every morning a report was made to Kiusko.

"This is the revelation which I came to sell you, and which I was not to make to you except for a large sum," he added, seeing my astonishment. "I have something in my pocket which will convince you, in case you have any doubts; it is the copy of the information given up to-day, including that of this morning, and droll enough reading it is."

He then drew from his pocket a bundle of papers, and gave them to me one by one. I read them. Day by day, hour by hour, I found recorded all that I had done for a week. Among other details were the following, from which you can judge of their exactness:

"Tuesday, the 7th, started on horseback from his hôtel at eight in the morning. Went directly to the Bois. At half-past eight met Count Kiusko near the bridge over the lake. Rode away together. At nine o'clock, joined by two gentlemen and two young ladies on horseback."—In the margin a note added: Commodore Montaigu, his daughters, and his nephew.—"At half-past ten, returned alone to the hôtel. Came out on foot at three. Went to the Rue de Monsieur. Left there at six o'clock. Took a cab and went to the club. At midnight left the club and returned to the Rue de Monsieur."

Two days later the report said:

"The hôtel in the Rue de Monsieur is inhabited by a Turk and his family, unknown at the embassy under the name of Omer-Rachid which he bears, and which must be false. Receives no letters by post. Never goes out except in a carriage, and in company with his three daughters, who are very young and very beautiful. Receives no visitors except M. André de Peyrade. The people in the neighborhood know only his name from the porter of the hôtel. *Incorruptible*."—This word, in parentheses, was underlined.—" The six female domestics, all foreigners, Turks or Greeks. The people in the stable and the coachmen alone are French. Know no more than the neighbors do. Never enter the house. It is a good place for them; well paid and the work easy."

I breathed a sigh of relief.

"Oh! don't be in such a hurry to rejoice," said Giraud. " Here is the report of to-day."

I took the last paper and read this astonishing discovery.

" The true name of Omer-Rachid is Mohammed-Aziz. He holds only a subordinate position in the house. The three young persons who inhabit the hôtel are not his daughters. He bought them at Constantinople on behalf of his master, who seems to be. M. André de Peyrade. They are called Hadidjé, Nazli, and Zouhra. The latter has commenced a flirtation by signs with a young officer living in the next house, and whose windows overlook the garden of the hôtel."

" What a ridiculous fable!" I cried, trying to conceal my dismay.

" So much the worse, then!" said Giraud. " It is a pity it is not true."

At the end of the report, were my actions of the previous evening, which terminated thus:

" At eleven o'clock, left the club and went to the Hôtel

de Téral, where he talked with a man who seemed to be awaiting him at the door."

"You see," said Giraud, "it is pretty accurate. While you were talking last night, your particular guardian angel was watching you."

On learning to what an extent this vile espionage had been carried, my first thought was to go and seek Kiusko. Such maneuvers were an insult to Kondjé-Gul as well as to me. I was not a man to let them pass without calling him severely to account. At the idea of my secrets being in the possession of a low spy, I felt mad with rage; but I reflected that it was important first of all to stop these last revelations, which were the gravest.

"The report of this morning has not yet been delivered to Count Kiusko?" I asked Giraud.

"No," he answered. "You are the only one who has seen it. That is what I was charged to sell you."

"Where is the man who sent you?"

"He is waiting for me in the cab at the corner of the street."

"Go find him, and bring him to me."

"What!" cried Giraud. "Are you going to fall into that rascal's trap? I should never dare to look you in the face again, for you would think that I had shared the booty with him. No! No! let me manage the affair! I will simply go to him and tell him that I am going to keep his little spy-report of this morning, and that if he ever dares to breathe a word to anyone, I'll choke the life out of him. And he will be silent, I promise you. He knows me!"

It was easy for me to make him understand that the knave might at any time escape him, and that the surest

means of forcing him to keep silence was to make it for
his interest to do so. Once compromised, too, by the bargain, of which Giraud would be the witness, and by
which he would deliver to me the proof of Kiusko's
actions, the Pole might be of use to me, if only to bear
testimony to the espionage, for which I intended to
demand reparation of the one who had employed him.

"What? Fight for that?" said Giraud, disdainfully.
"In your place, do you know what I should do? I would
content myself with quietly turning the tables on Kiusko
by employing his own spy, so that I could make him
believe whatever I wished."

Giraud was right. A duel between Kiusko and myself would compromise Kondjé-Gul. The reasons for it
could not be concealed.

"Beside," continued Giraud, "in case of misfortune
to you, you leave your enemy in the field. Now, since
you have motives to stop all curiosity, I will go and bring
you that scurvy knave, the Pole; only I do it on condition that I declare, before him, that I will touch no
part of his *honest* profits."

Half an hour afterward, the bargain was concluded,
and I had paid the price. The diplomate, who looks
like a gentleman, gave me two letters of Kiusko, by
showing which I shall have nothing to do but to
choose my hour and send him my seconds. Meanwhile, to put to rout his maneuvers, and to take
care that he does not employ surer spies, we have
arranged that Zarewski shall remain ostensibly in his
service. Each morning, he will receive his famous
reports, revised and corrected by me. Checkmate! You
can be assured he won't find out much. Of course, to-
day's report will be all in my favor. Omer-Rachid is

white as snow. "He lives quietly with his daughters. M. André de Peyrade is only a friend of his, who aids him in a serious work, which has something to do with politics, which explains their relations." Still, Giraud, who has not much confidence in the Pole, wishes now to remain his accomplice in order to watch him. He desires, he says, to study the detective system. He will, for form's sake, follow Kondjé-Gul, for Kiusko might possibly meet her in some place which his report would not mention. He would then perceive that he was being deceived, and would seek, perhaps, for a more faithful agent. This will help me, beside, to know the actions of Madame Murrah, whom I suspect.

This singular revelation could leave me no longer in doubt as to the obstinacy of Daniel's suit. He brought to the accomplishment of his project the unscrupulous savage energy of a will accustomed to see all things bow before it. The choice of means mattered little to a nature scarcely half tamed by an incomplete, education. Accustomed to act only as master, he followed up his end in view, crashing ahead and battering down all obstacles in his way. The suppleness of the Slav was clearly shown in this game, of which the happiness of his life was the stake. He loved Kondjé-Gul, as I knew, with a blind, unreasoning love. Rich or poor, he was ready to give her his name. Had he conjectured that the luxury of the two foreigners could not be based upon a very solid foundation? To penetrate the mystery with which he thought them surrounded, at the risk of losing his faith in Kondjé-Gul and of suffering the tortures of bitter disillusion, he did not recoil before a vile action which dishonored him. It even looked as if he hoped to discover some intrigue which would reanimate his hopes.

"Accessible to others," he thought, without doubt, "shall I not have a chance? Could she resist a bound-less love, dazzling wealth, and a marriage which would give her an unhoped-for position?" Strange as these deductions of mine were, Daniel's character and the words he had addressed to me, rendered them so logical, that I ended by becoming convinced of their truth.

Enlightened as to the maneuvers which gave me the explanation of his conduct, after the refusal he had received, I saw the folly of a meeting which would com-promise Kondjé-Gul, and perhaps give rise to a scandal; I held, moreover, the security of our secret in my hands. I was about to take my rival in his own trap, and mis-lead him by those very means he had so unscrupulously employed. It was evident that his suspicions were fixed upon me, but that he had no proof. These reflections calmed me. After all, was it not senseless to take um-brage at a pursuit which was only one of the thousand incidents I had foreseen. Kondjé-Gul's beauty must call forth passionate admiration? Why should I take notice of Kiusko more than any other? Informed of all his actions, I should, moreover, be on hand to intervene, and, if necessary, put an end to his hostile projects.

CHAPTER XXVIII.

Well! yes. It is true; I love her! You thought, I suppose, that I was going to deny it or try to conceal it as a weakness? Have I ever said that the effect of the loves of the harem was to suppress the heart and the soul and the thirst for the ideal? Where you seem to see a defeat, I glory in my happiness, and in the enchant-ing dream which I am experiencing wide-awake. Com-

pare the secret and charming tie which binds me to
Kondjé-Gul to the prosaic form of those vulgar *liaisons*
which display their cynicism to all eyes; or to those
shadowy love affairs which a remnant of hypocritical
virtue strives to conceal as a crime. Deceptive happiness, where possession always necessarily implies the
fall of the woman, and the loss of self-esteem in the man.
Preach or dogmatize as much as you like, to establish
the superiority of our social system over that of the
Orient, which you declare barbarous, you will never succeed in doing anything but entangling yourself in your
own paradoxes. In fact, in our state of civilization, all
illicit love is libertinism, and the woman who yields to it is
a polluted idol. Duchess or foolish virgin, you may
poetize her fall, but you can never forget it. The canker
is in the fruit. My love for Kondjé Gul knows neither
the shame nor the duplicity of vice. Proud of her sub-.
mission as a slave, she can love me without losing any of
her self-respect. In her eyes, her tenderness is legitimate;
her glory is to conquer my heart. I am her master, she
abandons herself to me without failing in any duty. A
daughter of Asia, she fulfills her destiny according to the
moral traditions and beliefs of her country, and she
remains faithful to them by loving me; her religion has
no other rule, her virtue no other law.

That is why I love her, why my heart has gone out to
her. You speak to me of the future, and you ask what
will happen when the day of my marriage to Anna Campbell arrives. The future is still far off, my dear fellow;
when the time comes, we shall see. Meanwhile, I love
her, I love her, I love her!

Are you satisfied? Yes, I confess my errors, I abjure
my pagan vanities, my sultanic principles. I deny Ma-

homet! I have found my road to Damascus, and the
true love has appeared to me in all its resplendent glory;
it has touched me with its grace, and my false idols
crumble into dust! Shall I make you a present of my
harem? If so, say the word, and I will send them to you
post haste; you can give them news of me, for it is six
weeks since I have seen my sultanas. Only make haste;
in eight days they depart for Constantinople. Civilization certainly did not agree with such little animals.
Their liberty in Paris ruined them. I secure them a
comfortable competency, and dismiss them.

CHAPTER XXIX.

Nothing apparently troubled our peace. Lent suspended for a time the round of gaiety, and our friendly
reunions gained thereby. The Hôtel de Téral was the
place most generally chosen. Maud and Suzannah liked to
go there, and Kondjé-Gul, like a child, was full of pride at
what she called her "reception days." Our little circle was
increased to a dozen people, carefully selected from their
young acquaintances. One or two mothers detracted nothing from the charm of our delightful evenings, and their
elegance and distinction did not prevent our gaiety. In
this more extended circle, Daniel's presence soon ceased
to trouble Kondjé-Gul; he, moreover, affected a light-
heartedness which showed no feeling of regret or rancor,
and his easy manners not differing from those of our
friend of former times, she concluded that he had sub-
mitted to his fate with a good grace, recognizing the
uselessness of a hope which could never be realized.

Both Kondjé-Gul and myself were thoroughly happy
in this quiet, domestic life. Her beauty seemed to

increase each day. We passed long evenings in those
pleasant tête-à-têtes, which are the sweetest hours for
hearts that love. I was very proud of my work, and I
contemplated with emotion the pure, ideal being whom
I had brought to life, and whose heart and soul I had
formed. The cultivation of her young mind, all full of
its Oriental beliefs, had produced a delightful contrast
of enthusiasm and judgment, which gave to the ingenuous expression of her new ideas the most original turn.
I was often surprised to find in her, mingled still with
her Asiatic superstitions, my secret sentiments, my most
foolish aspirations. It seemed indeed as if she only
thought, only lived in me, and that her tender emotions
had their source in my heart.

Our happiness was so assured, that it seemed to us
absurd to believe that it could be accessible to any attack.
Still, beneath all this peacefulness, a torturing thought
sometimes rose in my brain. Slight clouds passed over
the azure sky, and often, when with her, I thought
despite myself of the future, of the marriage which you
yourself have recalled to me, and from which nothing
can release me. However great the sacrifice must be,
it has never occurred to me not to fulfill my uncle's
wishes. I am bound by too many ties to this, my adopted
father, whose faith in my loyalty has been boundless;
I owe everything to this chivalrous benefactor, who left
his whole fortune in my hands, without even a suspicion
that I could be ungrateful crossing his mind, and,
although this duty to which I am resigned occasionally
makes me melancholy, I must confess it has only been a
fugitive impression. It has been harder to struggle with
a compromise of conscience, by which I have resolved to
reconcile my passion for Kondjé-Gul with my duties as

a husband. Anna Campbell's colorless character must certainly make of our union one of those contracts which it is our custom to call marriages of convenience, and the adorable secret of my love for Kondjé-Gul will always remain undiscovered. Moreover, if my uncle should possibly ever discover this relict of my Oriental life, he is certainly not a man to be angry, as long as all the laws of propriety are observed.

I gave myself up, therefore, without remorse, to the enjoyment of my tranquil life, when a new incident suddenly aroused all my anxiety.

One evening when I arrived a little late, because, of one of those wearisome dinners which mark Anna Campbell's issues from the convent, I found Kondjé-Gul looking very sad and with reddened eyelids. I had left her, a few hours before, joyous and delighted with a little pony I had presented her with that morning. Surprised and alarmed at so sudden a change, I anxiously questioned her. Something serious alone could have troubled the serenity of her happiness. At my first question, I saw that she wished to conceal from me the cause of her affliction. I persisted, and then she said:

"It is nothing; a story my mother told me."

But, as she tried to smile, a sob escaped from her lips. And, bursting into tears, she threw herself into my arms, hiding her head on my breast.

"Good heavens! What is it?" I cried in alarm. "I implore you, tell me all. What has happened? Why are you crying so?"

She could not answer me, but she seized my hand, which she covered with kisses, as if to protest her love in the midst of her sorrow.

"Kondjé-Gul, my darling," I exclaimed, divining that some fear had taken possession of her heart, "you know well how I love you, and that nothing can mar our happiness!"

I succeeded in calming her; then, making her sit down by me, I begged her to tell me her trouble. Her hesitation increased my anxiety; she turned away her eyes, and I saw that she did not dare to answer me. Finally, almost worried to death, I exerted my authority.

"Speak, I wish to know all," I said, mingling a certain firmness with my tenderness. "Whatever has happened, I order you to tell me your sorrow." I knew that she would not resist a formal expression of my will.

"You command it?" she said.

"I command you to tell me what your mother said, and why you have wept."

Then, with the submission of a child, she told me this strange story, which filled me with astonishment.

After breakfast, her mother had sought her in the *salon*, and, after some indifferent conversation, had commenced to speak to her of their country, their family, and how glad they would be to see them again after such a long absence. Kondjé-Gul let her speak on, taking these words only as one of those dreams of the distant future which the imagination caresses, in spite of the impossibility of their realization; but she was soon very much surprised to perceive that her mother considered this dream as likely soon to be accomplished. She questioned her. Then, with great reticence, Madame Murrah told her that she had learned that a marriage was decided upon between me and Anna Campbell, to whom I had been engaged for a long time, and that this marriage would take place in six months, and the day after the

wedding I would depart with my wife. The consequence of all these arrangements would be the abandonment of Kondjé-Gul.

I was dismayed at this unexpected revelation. The
project of my marriage was as yet a family secret, known
only to myself, to her, and to my aunt and uncle. How
could it have reached the ears of Madame Murrah?

"What!" I cried, thinking only of her sorrow. "Did
you think I could leave you, give you up, forget you?"

"This marriage is true, then?" she exclaimed, anxiously
gazing into my eyes.

"There is nothing true but our love!" I answered,
moved at her distress. "There is nothing true but my
wish to love you always, to defend our happiness, and to
live forever near you."

"But this marriage?" she repeated again.

It was no longer possible for me to recoil from
an avowal which I had intended to prepare her for
later.

"Listen to me, my darling," I said, taking her hands,
"and, above all, listen to me with confidence. I love you;
I love only you; it is you who are my wife, my happiness,
my life. Do you believe me?"

"Yes, I believe you. But she," she added, with a shudder, "Anna Campbell? You will marry her?"

"See," I said, wishing to calm her fears; "suppose, as
often happens in your country, I were forced, to assure
our happiness, to take another wife, would you not understand that it would be a sacrifice which I owe to my
uncle if he should exact it of me, a family arrangement
which could not separate us? What can you fear, if I
love only you? Were you worried about Hadidjé or
Zouhra, before they went away?"

"But they—they were not Christians! Anna Campbell will be your wife. Your religion and your law order you to love her."

"No," I cried, "neither my religion nor my law can change my heart or separate me from you. It is my duty to protect your life, to make you happy; are you not also my wife? Why should you be alarmed at an arrangement which would not trouble you, if we lived in your country? Anna Campbell does not love me; we are only two friends ready to accept one of those bonds of expediency, which you see all about you, which are only monetary transactions, and which demand only reciprocal esteem. My child, of what should you be jealous? Do you not know that you will always be all in all to me?"

Poor Kondjé-Gul listened to my words without a thought of disputing them. Still, under the yoke of her native ideas, the Oriental prejudices, in which she had been brought up, were too profoundly graven in her mind to permit our ideas and customs, often seeming to her so illogical, to brusquely convert her to a different appreciation of woman's destiny. According to her law and her religion I was her master. She could not understand the possibility of not yielding to my will; but I saw by her tearful eyes that her submission, so touching and so resigned, was only an effort of her tenderness, and that she suffered cruelly.

"Why do you weep?" I continued, taking her in my arms. "Have you any doubt of my heart?"

"Oh, no!" she exclaimed, quickly. "Why should I not believe you?"

"Then smile."

"Yes," she said, embracing me, "you are right, and I am foolish. What can you expect? I am still half bar-

barous, and I am a little dazed by all that I have learned
of your world. There are still things which I can not
understand. Why I am more jealous of Anna Campbell
than I was of Hadidjé, or Nazli, or Zouhra, I can not
tell, but I am afraid. She is a Christian; perhaps you
will love her differently from what you do me. It seems
to me that the law of your country is about to seize you,
and separate us. That odious law, which you revealed
to me once, which would set me at liberty, you said, if I
wished to leave you, returns often to my mind like a
ghastly horror. It seems to me that imaginary liberty,
which I do not wish, would become real, if you were to
marry."

I reassured her. The heart has an eloquence more
persuasive than the vain deductions of logic. In this
strange situation, where the conflict between her beliefs
and what she knew of our world alarmed my poor
Kondjé-Gul, I was myself sincere, deceiving myself as
to that compromise of conscience which appeared to me
to be imposed upon me by a strict duty. Singular as this
must appear to you, I have already lived too long the
life of the harem not to have been drawn little by little
into the current of Oriental ideas. The bond which
united me to Kondjé-Gul was, in my eyes, legitimate and
sacred. She was not my mistress; she was my wife.
Ought not the barbarian law which had given her to me,
the law of her country, which I had accepted, to protect her?

It was certain that the knowledge of my intended marriage to Anna Campbell could only have come to
Madame Murrah through Kiusko. His relationship to
my aunt had made him one of the family and he knew
our projects. It was easy for me to understand that his

jealous instinct had partially penetrated our secret. He had guessed, at least, that Kondjé-Gul loved me, and that I was an obstacle to his wishes. In pursuance of his object, he wished to destroy in advance all Kondjé-Gul's hopes, by revealing to her that I was affianced to another. Knowing his vile actions, I wondered uneasily, if in those chance or arranged interviews which he had had with Madame Murrah, some imprudent word had not betrayed all. For some days I thought I had noticed a certain reserve in him. It was possible that, convinced of the futility of his hopes, he only thought of vengeance by troubling at least the peace of his rival. My suppositions had reached this point, when a decisive event suddenly enlightened me.

CHAPTER XXX.

Tranquilized by my vows and promises for the future, Kondjé-Gul was too submissive to me not to have accepted a trial to which duty impelled me. Proud of sacrificing for me her jealousy, of giving up herself for my happiness, her tears were soon dried under my kisses, and the next day I found her as cheerful and trusting as if no cloud had dimmed our horizon; but, a few days afterward, I was surprised to detect a sort of sadness in her. Our happiness was so unalloyed that I attributed this to the annoyance her mother's peculiar temper at times caused her. But, as the days went by, I suspected that it was something more than a passing melancholy, and that she was tormented by some new anxiety which even my presence could not dissipate.

One evening, at one of our little gatherings at the Misses Montaigu's, Maud dragged me off to complete a
13

quadrille. As Kondjé-Gul never danced, as you know,
she retired into a little reception-room off the *salon*, and
busied herself with some albums. I was talking gaily to
Maud, when, in the glass over the fire-place, I perceived
Kiusko seated by Kondjé-Gul. It was quite natural
that, seeing her alone, he thought it his duty to join her.
It appeared to me, beside, from their looks, that their
conversation was on different subjects, and in that
slightly cold tone of intimacy which always reigned
between them. While talking, he turned over the leaves
of a keepsake. There was no reason why I should
occupy myself with this tête-à-tête, and I never even
thought of observing him, when, toward the end of the
quadrille, my eyes by chance rested upon Kondjé-Gul
and I saw her suddenly rise, as if some word of Daniel's
had annoyed her. It seemed to me that she blushed,
and, drawing herself up proudly, she appeared to answer
him in an irritated manner. When the dance was ended,
I left Maud, and, with some anxiety, I went to the reception-room. They were both standing. Kiusko had his
back to the door and did not see me enter, but Kondjé-
Gul perceived me.

"André," she said, "come here and give me your
arm."

At these strangely audacious words, Daniel could not
restrain a movement of the greatest astonishment; he
cast an amazed look at me. I advanced. She seized
my arm feverishly, and, addressing my rival, said:

"Count Kiusko, you have offered me your love for the
second time. This is why I refuse it: I am Monsieur
André de Peyrade's slave, and I love him!"

If a thunderbolt had fallen at Daniel's feet, he could
not have been more startled. He became so pale that I

thought he was going to faint. He looked at us both with a terrible light in his eyes, and his features contracted with such a savage expression that I instinctively placed myself between him and Kondjé-Gul. But, suddenly, doubtless frightened at his own fury, he made a gesture of despair and rushed out of the room.

Kondjé-Gul was trembling like a leaf.

"What has happened?" I asked.

"I will tell you all," she murmured; "but I am going home with my mother; come as soon as we have left."

Half an hour later I joined Kondjé-Gul at the Hôtel de Téral. She had dismissed Fanny and was waiting for me. When I entered, she threw her arms around my neck, and the tears, too long restrained, streamed from her eyes.

"What is it?" I cried.

And, taking her in my lap like a child, I put my arms around her.

"Listen," she said, recovering her self-control and speaking in a decided tone; "you must forgive me for what I have done; you must pardon me for having hidden my thoughts and sorrows from you in order not to afflict you."

"I pardon all," I said at once; "but speak quickly!"

"Well, for a week I have deceived you, telling you that nothing was the matter; that I did not know the reason of the sadness which I could not hide from you. I was afraid to anger you against my mother by telling you that it was she who tormented me."

"Your mother!" I cried; "what could she say to you?"

"You shall know all," she answered, eagerly, "for I must justify myself for having kept a secret from you.

You remember, do you not, that two weeks ago she
spoke to me of your marriage, saying that you were
going to leave me? I would not believe her. How
could she be informed of a project no one else knew of?
I represented to her that Anna Campbell being your
uncle's god-daughter, your friendship for her was quite
natural, almost a relationship, and to suppose a marriage
between you was absurd. It was only her motherly
anxiety that——"

"Yes, yes, I know; and then?"

"Then," continued Kondjé-Gul, throwing aside all
hesitation, "my mother told me that she had heard this
news from Count Kiusko, who had been informed by
your aunt."

"I was sure of it!" I cried; "but why did you not tell
me of this?"

"My mother made me promise to keep it a secret, because it was necessary, she said, that Count Kiusko
should have no suspicion of our love. She told me that
he attributed my refusal to be his wife to the hope I
doubtless had of a marriage with you."

"Continue! Come to what has happened since."

"You know in what sorrow you found me that evening. I could not hide my tears from you, and you ordered me to tell you the reason of them. Finally, you
were so kind that I thought only of you. Happy to
sacrifice myself to your will, I forgot the next day my
fears, with which I reproached myself as an offense
against our love. I told my mother all your kind words,
and I imagined that I had reassured her. A few days
after, I was very much astonished to hear her return to
the same subject; she had seen the count again, who
this time had declared to her that your uncle would dis-

inherit you if you disobeyed his wishes; that he was about to depart for India, where he intended to take you with him and fix his residence there, as he did not desire to live longer in France."

"And you believed that?"

"No," she answered, quickly; "you had not told me of it! But, seeing that I would believe only you, my mother one day changed her tone; she spoke to me of Count Kiusko; of his wealth and his love."

"She did that?"

"Oh! pardon her!" she exclaimed. "She is so anxious for me and for herself; she fears the future. She imagines me abandoned by you! Finally, three days ago, something, I know not what, happened at your aunt's reception; for, when we returned here, my mother said to me, in a resolute tone, that she had decided to live no longer in the midst of infidels, and that she wished to return to the country of the faithful to expiate so great a crime. I was dismayed at this determination; it had its source in our faith, and I could not oppose it, for that would have been sacrilege; but I could at least appeal to her tenderness, beg her not to leave me. Then, while I was on my knees before her, she said to me these frightful words: 'You will not quit me when I go, for I shall take you with me!'"

"She is mad!" I cried.

"You understand, do you not," continued Kondjé-Gul, the blow this was to me? I fell, almost senseless. My mother was alarmed and called Fanny. The next day, I implored her again, declaring that it would kill me to separate me from you. I thought I had softened her, for, she said, embracing me, that she wished only my happiness. But that evening, when we were in the

carriage going to Suzannah's, she spoke to me again of
Count Kiusko. Some presentiment told me that the
greatest enemy of our love was he; that it was he who
influenced and guided my mother, with some thought of
revenge, perhaps; that he hoped, doubtless, that, separated
from you, I could no longer resist my mother. You
know the rest; I entered the reception-room while you
were dancing, and he came and sat down by me. ' Is
it true that you are going away?' he said, after a moment.
' What can make you think that?' I answered, coldly.
' Some words of your mother's gave me to understand
such was the case.' I kept silence; he did not dare to
go on, and for some moments said not a word. I did
not turn my eyes from the book I was examining, but I
felt that his gaze was fixed upon me. 'You would
regret André, perhaps,' he said, at last; ' but what does
that matter? He is not free, even if he loved you.' At
these words, whose cruel irony I felt, a mad thought
crossed my brain; I raised my head, and answered him
so haughtily that he rose in confusion. At that moment
you entered. I wished to load him with my contempt,
and cut off forever all his hopes. You know what I
said."

"You did well; for it was necessary to end it. I will
take care of him hereafter."

"But if my mother wishes to separate us?"

"Your mother!" I cried. "Would your mother, who
sold you, delivered you up as a slave, dare to claim the
rights she has lost?"

"Could you defend me against her?"

"Yes; I will defend you," I cried, with rage, "if I
have to carry you away, to fly with you so far that she
can never find any trace of you."

"Oh! I will follow you," she exclaimed, excitedly. "Save me! I could not live without your love!" "Good!" I answered, seizing her hand. "And now calm yourself. There is, at the bottom of all this, a miserable scheme, of which nothing will remain to-morrow, for I am about to destroy it. I am going to seek Count Kiusko, and he shall never trouble you again, I promise you; then I will see your mother."

"Ah!" cried Kondjé-Gul. "Are you going to fight?"

"No, no," I answered, laughing to remove all fear. "But you understand that an explanation is necessary between us."

CHAPTER XXXI.

In the morning, I put my affairs in order to be ready for any event, and then I sought two of my friends, whom I asked to hold themselves in readiness to serve as my seconds in an affair which grave circumstances might force me to settle that very day. Assured of their coöperation, I repaired to Kiusko's apartments in the Rue de l'Elysée. When I reached the house, I saw, from the open shutters, that he was up. A servant who knew me was in the court-yard, and he told me that he did not think his master was visible. I gave him my card and requested him to take it at once to the count. After a few moments, he returned and begged me to go up to his master's apartments; he ushered me into a little smoking-room, adjoining the bed-room, and where only intimate friends were admitted. Daniel at once appeared, dressed in a sort of Moldavian costume.

"Ah! is it you, my dear André," he said, in an easy

tone, and with an affectation of calmness which his pallor contradicted.

He held out his hand and I took it; he then seated himself, motioning me to a chair on the other side of the fire-place.

"What good fortune brings you here so early in the morning?" he said, with a puff at his cigar.

"You expected me, I suppose?" I replied, looking him full in the face.

He sustained my gaze steadily, with a smile on his lips.

"I expected you, and I did not expect you, I may say."

By the manner in which this was said, I saw that he was resolved to force me to speak first of the object of my visit.

"So be it!" I said, wishing to show him that I guessed his thought. "I will explain."

"Go on, my dear fellow," he replied.

"I have come to speak to you," I continued, distinctly, "of Mademoiselle Kondjé-Gul Murrah, and of what took place last evening between you and herself."

"Ah! I understand; in regard to the somewhat startling reprimand I drew upon myself, and the disclosure she made to me."

"Exactly," said I; "you have admirably summed up the whole matter in those two words; a reprimand and a disclosure. Now, as it results, from the second, that I am responsible for all Mademoiselle Murrah's actions, I have come to place myself at your disposal, on account of the reprimand she saw fit to give you."

"What folly, my dear fellow!" he cried, blowing a ring of smoke into the air. "After all, I only received what I deserved, and my own presumption alone is to blame. The wrath of so beautiful a person is certainly a great misfortune for him who excites it, and my only regret is that I have displeased her. The idea of holding you responsible for that little incident is simply ridiculous; strictly speaking, I should even say that it was my place to apologize, if I could not plead the complete ignorance in which you left me as to the mysterious relations existing between you, which would have been an obstacle in the way of the plans I had confided to you."

I understood the veiled irony and censure contained in these last words, but I was no longer troubled with any remorse, as far as he was concerned.

"So," I said, "you have nothing to say to me, nothing to demand of me on the subject of that reprimand?"

"Absolutely nothing, my dear fellow," was his reply, in that easy tone he had assumed throughout. "And I think that nothing could be more absurd than a disagreement, on that account, between two friends like us."

"Very well," I said, imitating his coolness. "Since you take it so amicably, I will not persist. But, the first point settled, we must speak of what you call the disclosure."

At this, he could not repress a slight start. A gleam appeared in his eyes, but it was only for a moment.

"Oh! yes," he said, carelessly; "now for the second point."

"That is the one which is of importance to me," said I, "and I must ask you what you intend to do after such a revelation?"

"Simply to congratulate you, my dear fellow, on your astonishing good fortune. What? that beautiful young girl, whom we have viewed, in her enchanting grace, moving like a queen in the most aristocratic *salons* of Paris and arousing the greatest admiration, is your slave?   Acknowledge that there is no mortal in the world who would not envy you."

" Do your congratulations imply a promise to renounce your pretensions, which you now know to be useless?"

" But, my dear friend," he exclaimed, laughing, " are you going to ask me now to give you my confidence? In that case, I must recall to you that beautiful Panurge illustration which you cited to me the other day, to show me the folly of those who ask and those who give advice.   Then, refusing to assist me with your knowledge, and apparently uninterested in my foolish intentions, you tried to correct my ridiculous Russian artlessness. And now, to-day, you want to question, counsel, and guide me, as if you were my guardian, or as if Panurge had never dilated upon affairs of the heart.   The devil! Permit me to say that you are exceedingly illogical."

Exasperated by his imperturbable *sang-froid*, which I could not disturb, I exclaimed, looking him in the eyes: " Kiusko, are you determined not to understand me?"

" Oh! my friend," he replied, with an odd smile, " I understand perfectly that you wish to quarrel with me and force me to demand of you a satisfaction, which I do not appear sufficiently to desire; but, between ourselves, I assure you that that would look to me like folly."

" Do you understand, at least," I exclaimed, " that I forbid you to make any further advances to Mademoiselle Kondjé-Gul Murrah?"

" Fie! Fie! What do you take me for? After such an astonishing revelation from her, I should be lacking in the commonest attributes of a gentleman if I did not entirely relieve her of my presence; so you need give yourself no further anxiety on that point."

" Do you mean by that evasive response that you will hereafter give up your maneuvers with her mother, which I might perhaps qualify in a manner you would not like to listen to?"

"Good heavens! you must see the game would be too unequal! And I do not think the good lady would be much help, after what I know now. Beside," he added, " you have given me your confidence as a friend, and, tardy as it may be, it binds me henceforth, were it only out of that regard which should exist between relations in serious matters."

I thought for a moment of hurling in his face the name of the Pole, Zarewski; but I saw clearly that he was playing a treacherous rôle, and that it would be dangerous to commit such an imprudence.

"Well, my dear Daniel," I said, rising, " I see, in any case, that you are very good-natured."

" Am I not?" he replied; " and yet some people reproach me with having a bad temper!"

CHAPTER XXXII.

The most formidable dangers are those which one instinctively feels, without being able to discern either the enemy or the snare laid. My interview with Kiusko left me with a feeling amounting almost to terror. I knew too well his bravery, not to understand that his passiveness under insult could be only the cold calculation of an implacable will, which would pursue its purpose of passion, vengeance, or hatred with all the energy of despair. Despite the humiliation he had undergone, I felt that he had not abandoned his design. He was determined to have Kondjé-Gul by stratagem, or by violence, if needs be. Remembering his frightful calmness, which

seemed only to bide its time, I wondered if some plot
was not already on foot against us. However, I was not
a man to be weakened by puerile fears, and I soon overcame my passing emotion. I knew that, after all, the
struggle was too unequal for me to have any doubts as
to the results. However resolved Kiusko might be not
to abandon the cowardly part he had been playing, I
could always force him to fight, by publicly insulting
him. Once reassured by this thought, I determined to
regulate my line of conduct by the result of the interview I was about to have with Kondjé Gul's mother. I
must have a clear understanding with Madame Murrah,
who was unconsciously, perhaps, an accomplice in projects, whose aim she did not comprehend. It was eleven
o'clock, and knowing that I should find her alone, as
Kondjé-Gul would be busy with her lessons, I went to
the Hôtel de Téral.

As I reached there, a carriage stopped before the
door and Madame Murrah alighted. She seemed a little
disconcerted at seeing me. Considerably surprised that
she had gone out so early, I asked her to enter the *salon*.
She did so, and, seeing me take a chair, she seated herself upon the divan with her accustomed indolence, and
waited for me to speak.

There is no doubt but that, according to our ideas, my
dear Louis, the scene I am about to relate to you is a
strange one. I shall tell it to you as it happened; but
you must not forget that the Circassian saw nothing in
it opposed to the principles and ideas of her race.

" I have come to speak to you," I began, " on a very
serious subject, and to which, doubtless, you have not
given much thought. But, without meaning to, you
have caused Kondjé-Gul much sorrow."

" How could I cause my daughter sorrow?" she inquired, as though she failed to understand.

" By constantly repeating to her that I was about to leave her and be married; by telling her that you wished to return home, and even that you had decided to take her with you. She is unnecessarily alarmed at all this."

" If it is written by Allah," she said, tranquilly, " who can prevent it?"

I expected denials, evasions; but these fatalistic words falling coldly from her lips startled me.

" But Allah can not order you to cause your daughter's unhappiness," I replied, sternly.

"You are about to marry."

"What matters my marriage?" I rejoined. "It can in no way trouble Kondjé-Gul's happiness. She knows that I love her and that she will always be the first in my affections."

Madame Murrah shook her head.

" Your wife will be an infidel," she said, " and, according to your law, she can demand the abandonment of my daughter."

Thunderstruck at hearing her use such arguments, when I thought all I had to do was to give her my orders, I gazed at her in amazement.

" But my wife will never know of Kondjé-Gul!" I cried. " She will live in her own house, and Kondjé-Gul here, without any change."

At this speech the Circassian reflected for an instant, as if not knowing how to answer me. But suddenly, just as I thought I had convinced her, she said:

"All you have said to me would do very well if we were in Turkey; but you know better than I that in your country your religion does not permit you to have but one wife."

"But," I exclaimed, more and more astonished at her language, "do you think Kondjé-Gul would ever doubt my honor and loyalty?"

"My daughter is a child who believes everything," she answered. "But I have consulted a lawyer, and I have learned that, according to your laws, she is as free as any French woman, and that consequently she has lost all the rights of *cadine* which she would have in our country. I have learned, finally, that you could leave her without her having any claims upon you."

I was literally stunned at these words and at the expression of her face as she gave utterance to them. Here was no longer the apathetic Oriental, whom I thought I could command as a master, but another woman, decided, resolute, defiant.

"When your lawyer told you that your daughter was free," said I, changing my tone in my turn, "he doubtless also informed you that you could marry your daughter to Count Kiusko."

"Oh! I knew that before he told me," she responded, with a smile.

"So, for two months, you have deceived me by making me believe that you had answered him by a refusal."

"It was necessary to prevent you from telling him what he knows now. That foolish Kondjé-Gul informed him of the truth yesterday."

"How do you know that?"

She blushed.

"I know it. That is sufficient!" she answered, boldly.

"May I ask you what you intend to do, now that Count Kiusko knows all?" I inquired, controlling my anger.

"I shall do what I consider best for my daughter's happiness. You can not marry her without being obliged to give up your uncle's fortune. If Count Kiusko should still wish to make her his wife, despite what he knows, you can see that, as a mother, I could only approve of a marriage which would assure her so wealthy a future."

At these words I lost all control of myself.

"Ah!" I cried. "And do you think that I will allow you to dispose of her like that and not defend her?"

"Yes, yes; I know that also. And it is precisely in regard to that that I consulted the lawyer; but, from what he told me, what authority have you over my daughter? What right can you appeal to as against mine?"

"But you must foresee, also, I suppose, that I can ruin your hopes of wealth by killing Count Kiusko," I exclaimed, beside myself with rage.

"If it is written!" she repeated, coldly.

Exasperated at this fatalistic unconcern, all sorts of thoughts of fury and violence mounted to my brain. I rose and walked to and fro to calm myself. I saw that for two months past I had been the dupe of this woman; that she was eagerly pursuing a hope of unlooked-for fortune from which nothing could turn her aside. I felt as though I were caught in a trap.

Motionless upon the divan, with her hands clasped in her lap, she silently watched me.

"Look here," I said, turning toward her, "your maternal solicitude has its foundation in a question of money. For what sum will you sell me your daughter for the second time, and return alone to the East?"

I saw a gleam in her eyes, and she opened her lips to answer me, but a moment's reflection caused her to hesitate.

"I will tell you in a week," she said, at last.

I guessed that she still had some hope in Kiusko, and that she probably wished to wait until she was sure on that point, but I considered it prudent to say no more.

Events had followed one another so rapidly since the evening before that I wondered if I were awake. Kondjé-Gul's revelation of her mother's duplicity, my explanation with Daniel, and finally this cynical discussion, in which the Circassian had declared to me boldly her plans, all this had so brutally struck, blow upon blow, my peaceful happiness, that I could scarcely realize my misfortune. Overcome with fear at the idea that I might lose Kondjé-Gul, I thought I should become insane. I fought with all my strength against my despair. I had been foolishly confident of the future, and had never dreamed anyone could take Kondjé-Gul away from me. I had lived on, foolishly believing that I could put an end with my sword, when the time came, to my rival's vain presumptions. And I now awoke in consternation, caught in the stupid trap I had allowed to be set for my feet. Kondjé-Gul's mother had been made Kiusko's accomplice. How could I foil this plot of two ardent, pitiless, and resolute passions, which would recoil, as I now knew, before no violence or treachery. I was powerless, disarmed, before this miserable woman, who had only to claim her authority over her daughter to coerce her and dispose of her life. She could take her and carry her away from me, but I could, at least, bar Daniel's path and prevent him from joining her.

Suddenly an idea occurred to me. Was it not senseless of me to abandon myself to these puerile fears, and wait till the Circassian and Kiusko should make some concerted movement? Could I not fly, bear away Kondjé-Gul, and hide her from all pursuit?

This thought once entered into my head, it fixed itself there, and in a few minutes became a resolve. I was astonished that it had not occurred to me sooner, and I decided to put it into execution that very day. I knew that Kondje-Gul would joyfully follow me, happy to go and live alone with me in some quiet place. We had often spoken of such a project, which I had promised her some day to realize.

To assure the success of our flight, I resolved not to tell her till the last moment, for fear that she would inadvertently cause her mother to suspect something. I was to dine with her alone at the Hôtel de Téral. At eight o'clock I would order the carriage as if for a drive in the Bois. At half-past eight we would depart for Italy. I chose Capri as our destination. From there, I would make terms with her mother, without disclosing the place of our retreat.

Recovered from my alarm, and certain as to the issue of this struggle, in which my life and happiness were at stake, I returned home, in order to see my uncle and tell him I was going away. My valet would be sufficient for us on our journey. I gave him orders to be at the railway station with the luggage, before our arrival; and now I am waiting for evening, thinking of our delightful journey and of Kondjé-Gul's joy when I tell her that I am going to carry her off.

CHAPTER XXXIII.

Louis, a terrible misfortune has fallen upon my head! I am overwhelmed, crushed! I write to you a prey to

14

despair. My groans and cries of rage stifle me. Kondjé-
Gul is lost to me! Lost! Lost! Do you understand that
frightful word? Can you comprehend my sorrow? And
I still live! My God! how is it possible?

I must relate to you the disaster. Imagine the most
infamous and most unexpected blow striking me to the
heart, at the very moment I thought I had conquered in
the struggle. But my lamentation will give you no
information; I must tell you all so that you can understand me.

You know that yesterday I had made all my preparations to fly with Kondjé-Gul. My orders were given
and our departure resolved upon. A little before the
dinner hour, I went to the Hôtel de Téral. She had
gone out with her mother and had not yet returned. I
waited without worrying at a delay which a call could
explain. But when the clock in the *salon* struck half-
past seven I was astonished. I called Fanny and questioned her; she knew nothing.

"You did not hear mademoiselle say that she would
be late to-day?" I asked her.

"Mademoiselle said nothing, monsieur," was her reply.

"The butler knows I am to dine here?"

"Yes, monsieur, and he is only waiting mademoiselle's
return to serve dinner."

"Did mademoiselle go out at her usual hour?"

"No, monsieur," answered Fanny. "She did not intend
to go out at all, for no order had been given to the coachman; but, about six o'clock, a letter was brought here, and
Madame Murrah gave orders to have a cab called, as
she did not wish to wait to have our horses harnessed."

"To whom was this letter addressed?"

"To Madame Murrah; I delivered it to her myself."

"And they both went out?"

"Yes, monsieur."

"Very well," I said. "I will wait."

I thought some message from Maud or Suzannah had doubtless summoned her. The delay would cause us to lose the train, but I reflected that that was of no great moment as we could take the next one, which would carry us sufficiently far that night, and the next day we could continue our journey.

Still the moments rolled by. At eight o'clock, I began to be uneasy. Such a delay was strange; some accident, perhaps, had happened. I rang and sent a messenger to the commodore's. My carriage was at the door and the servant took it. In a quarter of an hour he brought me back word from Suzannah that she had not seen Kondjé-Gul all day. I was exceedingly alarmed at this, but I still waited. The hands of the clock marked half-past eight, then nine. I had exhausted all conjectures. I questioned Fanny in vain. Uneasy as myself, she knew nothing.

Suddenly a horrible thought seized me. I ran to Kondjé-Gul's chamber, trembling at the fear of finding there some indication of a sudden departure. There was no sign that she had left it in any trouble. Upon her writing-desk were a few unfinished lines, in answer to a note from Maud, accepting an invitation to ride in the Bois the next morning. It was evident that she had been interrupted by the arrival of the letter which Fanny had mentioned.

I hastened to Madame Murrah's room; I might perhaps discover some traces of the mystery there. The door was locked; I burst it open with my foot. Everything was in its accustomed order; no change, nothing to show a hasty determination. Some jewels upon the mantel-piece, a dressing-gown thrown on the bed. Upon the work-table was a piece of embroidery with the needle in it, a string of beads, and a Turkish book containing prayers and verses from the Koran. Nothing showed the least preparation for an absence of even a day. It was impossible to believe in a flight.

I returned to the *salon;* it was nearly ten o'clock. Wild with anxiety, I thought of going in search of her; but where was she? Whither should I direct my steps? Had some serious accident occurred? How could I explain the fact, if such were the case, that neither her mother nor herself had been able to send to the hôtel and inform me of it? Suddenly the idea came to me that some stratagem had been employed. Was not this letter, which had come half an hour before my arrival, and had seemingly determined their going out, a trap? Kiusko, alone, could be at the bottom of it. I recalled my interview with him during that morning, his evasive responses, his cowardice under my insults. Without any doubt he had been playing a part to turn aside my suspicions. He was meditating then an infamous project; but how to checkmate him! What could I do after so long a time had elapsed since Kondjé-Gul's departure? The mother was his accomplice, and they were dragging her away from me, while I, like a fool, was waiting at the hôtel for her return.

Mad with rage, I suddenly remembered that there was one sure way of finding some trace of them. Kiusko had not abandoned his vile espionage. I had received that morning the report of the previous day. Kondjé-Gul and her mother must have been followed; but where and how to find at once the man who had done so? Would it not be too late if I waited till the next day? But perhaps Giraud had already seen him! It was more than eleven o'clock, and perhaps Giraud was at home.

I jumped into my carriage, which was before the door.

In a quarter of an hour, I reached the Rue Serpente; the *concierge* told me Giraud had not yet returned. Fortunately, she knew his habits, and she directed me to a café, where he might be. I hastened there, and, on entering, I discovered him playing billiards; but, doubtless guessing that some unfortunate event had brought me there, he threw down his cue at once, and drawing me aside, inquired anxiously:

"What has happened?"

Without my having confided anything to him, he had some time since discovered my secret. In a few words I acquainted him with my reason for seeking him.

"There must be some rascality underneath this," he said. "But we shall know all before long. Joseph is sharp, discreet, and faithful. He comes every evening before midnight to bring me the notes which you revise in the morning."

"Who is this Joseph?"

"He is a hair-dresser, and lives in the Quartier Latin. The poor devil was out of a place, and I suggested him to the Pole, because I was sure of him, and I knew that he would never let out more than I told him to. But there he is now. Follow me; he will join us on the boulevard."

We left the café, and a moment afterward his emissary appeared.

"You can speak before this gentleman," said Giraud; "he is my friend. Come, quickly give us to-day's report."

"Faith, Monsieur Giraud, it won't take long," replied Joseph, "and I shan't need to write it out for you."

"Good! So much the better; go on!"

"Well, this is my report. At ten o'clock in the morning, Madame Murrah went out alone on foot. She took a cab in the Champs-Elysées and drove to the Rue de l'Elysée. A servant in livery, who was standing in the doorway, told me that the house was inhabited by Count Kiusko. The lady reappeared at half-past eleven and returned directly home."

I was astounded to hear this. At the very hour I called on Daniel, Kondjé-Gul's mother was there. She was there during our interview, and did not leave till a quarter of an hour after me.

"Continue," said Giraud. "Come to this evening."

"At half-past six, Madame Murrah came out, this time with her daughter, and entered a hired carriage which she had sent for. I hailed a cab and followed them. They went directly to the Eastern railway station. They had no luggage. Without taking tickets, they passed through the private door which leads to the platform. A train was to leave in ten minutes; I ran to the window and purchased a ticket. Five minutes afterward I was upon the platform; I examined all the carriages, but could not discover them; I remained upon the platform, but they did not appear, and the train left. I thought that they might possibly have come to meet someone whom they expected to arrive; I went to the waiting-rooms, but there was no one there. I then questioned one of the train-hands, who told me that he had indeed seen the two ladies I described, some ten minutes before, but that they had immediately left by a special train, ordered for themselves alone. He could not tell me their destination. I waited at the station till now, but they did not return. And here I am!"

You can understand my feelings during this recital. Left alone with Giraud, I gave reins to my excitement. Kondjé-Gul was gone! How had they deceived her? How could I find their traces? But Kiusko at least remained to wreak my vengeance upon.

"Come! Come!" exclaimed Giraud. "You must not touch a hair of his head. He is the one who will help us to find her."

He was right.

"Listen," he continued; "after what you once did for me, despite the way you met me again, you must know that you can command me to any extent. I can now render you a service, and I have friends, who are good fellows, and whom I can trust as I would myself. Will you give me *carte-blanche?* I promise you that in a week we shall have news. I would bet my head on it. Only, you must leave me to act; afterward, you can do what you like to your Russian."

I agreed to everything; but first it was necessary to be sure that Kiusko had not disappeared. When I expressed my fears on this subject to Giraud, he said:

"No, no! he is too sharp for that. It would be a great mistake for him to disappear the same day."

My carriage was two steps off, and we entered it and drove to the Rue de l'Elysée. We prudently stopped some distance from the house, and Giraud went in search of information. After a few minutes, he returned.

"As I foresaw," he said, "the count is still here. I invented a pretext to ask for him. He is at the club; go there to make certain, but above all be calm; no folly! appear to ignore all."

A quarter of an hour afterward, I entered the club. As I glanced in a mirror, I perceived that I was very pale. I had eaten no dinner, and I was faint with hunger. Before going to the card-rooms, where Kiusko must be, I ordered a bottle of port, of which I drank several glasses, one after the other, to revive me and enable me to conceal my emotion. Then I went to the *baccarat*-room. Kiusko was there, keeping the bank.

"Ah! there you are, André," he exclaimed gaily, as I appeared. "Come and stand behind my chair to give me luck. I am losing like the devil!"

I answered with a laugh. There was no change in his face; he was as thoroughly at his ease as if he knew nothing, and nothing had taken place between us. After remaining a few minutes, I took my departure and joined Giraud, who was waiting for me.

"Well, now that you are easy as regards him," he said, "let me take your carriage. I want to make haste and I am working for you. Don't worry; you have not to deal this time with the Pole, and you are going to be aided by people as devoted to me as I am to you, men, whose hearts and heads have been proved.

CHAPTER XXXIV.

Fifteen days have passed. Fifteen days of unutterable anguish. Have I still my reason? I can not tell. My life seems arrested, and this suspense is torture. Fool! while in possession of my happiness, I thought I knew how much I loved her! And my despair is doubled when I think of what my poor Kondjé Gul must suffer far away from me. Where have they taken her? What is she doing? I know nothing and I am waiting. For what? I am waiting for the departure of Kiusko, whom I watch like a cat. If he should escape me! They have doubtless carefully concealed her; their vile plot attests that; precautions were taken to hide from me the last vestige of her whereabouts. At times, I am seized by horrible fears. If I should be vanquished in the end? I may discover where she is. But what then? How can I rescue her from their hands?

All this must seem to you like delirium, and so it is, but it is a delirium which is killing me, and your kind heart is the only one I can cry out to.

This is what has happened during the last two weeks: Giraud and two of his friends, as much to be relied upon as himself, aided by Joseph, have been on foot night and day. Kiusko is surrounded by a network, no mesh of which can be broken. Despite his affectation of continuing his usual life, as if decided to remain indefinitely in Paris, I have now the proof that it was he who did all. I can assure you, I have no scruples now! The day after Kondjé-Gul's abduction, Giraud bribed one of Kiusko's servants. We have received from him the following dispatch, dated Strasburg, and which Daniel had left on his desk.

"Arrived safely. Found the one waiting us. Shall leave at once.   MURRAH."

Alas! Boundless despair takes strange consolation. This dispatch confirmed my worst fears, but it gave me news of her. It dissipated the profound darkness in which I had been groping. I read it over ten times, as if, having thought her dead, I had learned at last that she was living. I had feared lest she had entirely disappeared without leaving me any clue which could guide

me; I had even feared lest it should not be Kiusko's
work; I knew now that through him I should find her.

Since that dispatch we have had no news. I do not
know how I live. All day long I wait, hoping for a letter from her, a word which she might be able to confide
to some hôtel servant or railway employé. Nothing!
Sometimes I imagine that she has managed to escape,
that she has returned to the Hôtel de Téral, and I hasten
there. Alas! the hôtel is ever empty, and everything
there reminds me of my lost happiness, which increases
my suffering.

And then I have to conceal my distress from all eyes.
To explain my pallid and haggard countenance, I say
that I am suffering from a pain in my heart. Ah! I do
not lie! My poor uncle is alarmed, and my aunt is very
anxious about me. Very clear-sighted, she, perhaps, has
guessed something, for she has never ventured to say a
word to me of Kondjé-Gul. When Maud and Suzannah
come to the house, I can not bear to see them. The
inexplicable disappearance of their friend has greatly
saddened them. Her silence astonishes them; when
they speak of her it drives me mad. I have no strength
except in Kiusko's presence. Ah! How I shall kill him
some day! But his life is too precious to me at present.

Where can she be now? From Strasburg, her mother
may have gone to Vienna, to return to Turkey by the
Danube and Varna. Once there, Kondjé-Gul is
defenceless.

I open my lettter to tell you that an hour ago Kiusko
called upon my aunt. I was present. During the conversation he carelessly spoke of "business" which would
necessitate, perhaps, his near departure for Italy—that is,
in the course of a couple of weeks.

CHAPTER XXXV.

Kiusko has quitted Paris! As I expected, he disappeared suddenly one night, a week before his appointed time. He left alone with his valet, leaving orders to the rest of his household to return to Bessarabia. My aunt received a letter the next day from him, making his excuses and farewells, and in which he says that bad news compelled his sudden departure. But Giraud was on the watch, left with him, and the next day was joined by his friends. They will follow him to the ends of the world if necessary. They are furnished with plenty of money, and they journey separately, and apparently as if they did not know each other. If Kiusko escapes one of them, another will be on hand. He took the Lyons Railway. On the second day, a dispatch informed me of his arrival at Marseilles. His valet had engaged staterooms in the packet-boat for Naples, which was to start the next day. Perhaps he intends from Naples to embark at Messina on the Constantinople steamer.

It is doubtless there that Kondjé-Gul's mother is awaiting him. The barbarity of the Turkish laws alone can aid them to accomplish their cowardly designs.

CHAPTER XXXVI.

He stopped at Genoa; then he went to Milan, where he remained three days; from there he wrote to my aunt, asking her to answer him at the Hôtel de la Ville, but he departed for Venice and Trieste. My last dispatch is from Leybach, and he seems to be mak-

ing for Vienna. Why has he taken this roundabout
way, and why did he write that letter giving a false address, if not to baffle suspicion?

I have this moment received further news. He went
to Vienna, and from there embarked on the Danube. He
is evidently going to join them.

A few lines which I have received from Giraud,
reassure me, however. I can 'rely, he says, upon his
friends as upon himself. Brave hearts! Will they succeed in saving her?

CHAPTER XXXVII.

Three weeks have gone by since my last letter, and
all our conjectures are at fault. Kiusko is in Bessarabia, in one of his castles, a few leagues from Kichenau,
on the banks of the Dniester, and no trace of Kondjé-
Gul has been discovered. He lives there, hunting and
entertaining with great magnificence, without any of his
actions being in the least suspicious, and it is impossible
that the fugitives can be hidden in the neighborhood.
It must be that in aiding the abduction, his motive was
one of vengeance alone by destroying the happiness of
the one who had spurned him, and that the deed once
accomplished, he thinks no more of it. However, I
hold myself in readiness for any event. One of Giraud's
two friends, who accompanied him, managed to become
acquainted with Kiusko on the steamer. Speaking four
or five languages, he gave himself out as a civil engineer
on his way to examine the mines of the country. Kiusko
invited him to stay at the castle and hunt with him. In
the heart of the enemy's camp, he sends me almost
every day the most precise details. There is no woman

in the castle except an old relative of the count; she
mingles but little in the gaiety going on there.

I am still waiting, ready to depart at the first signal,
but I do not dare to budge yet. Suppose she should
return and find me away! I pass all my days at the
Hôtel de Téral.

CHAPTER XXXVIII.

Alas! It is now three months since she disappeared!
You can imagine what I suffer in this horrible suspense.
Day follows day and——

Frightful news has reached me, and they are discovered! The woman at the castle is Madame Murrah.
Kondjé-Gul is shut up in a convent. Kiusko has announced to his friends his approaching marriage.

I leave at once!

CHAPTER XXXIX.

I write to you from Khorestakh, a little town a few
leagues from Pruth and the Turkish frontier, where I
arrived yesterday. Giraud was waiting for me with his
companions. He had scarcely mentioned them to me,
and I acknowledge I was surprised to meet two men
as intelligent as himself. They are already my friends,
and I certainly could not wish for more devoted ones,
in the desperate enterprise I have undertaken to save
Kondjé-Gul. One of them, a short, heavily-built Breton,
is named Jacquet; he is a medical student, and supports
himself, while pursuing his studies, by reading the proof
of a daily paper. The other, Jean Dumont, is a chemist,
attached to the laboratory of a great manufactory. He
thinks he can make a fortune in this country, and already

has a scheme in his head. Compelled, like Giraud, to struggle for their daily bread, and attached to him by that true friendship often made in the schools, they have formed themselves, it appears, into a sort of cœnaculum, of which Giraud is the high priest. Giraud told them that he was paying a debt of honor, and that he needed their aid; so they followed him, delighted to play the part of knights-errant. Dumont is the one who knows Kiusko, whom they always call among themselves " the odious kidnapper." My courage has returned at sight of their confidence. They enjoy the idea of fighting against feudal oppression, and they bring to their work all that enthusiasm and valiant energy which is a gage of success.

Hope has revived me, and, delivered from that inertia which was killing me, I shall find at least in action a few days' respite from my despair. If I fail, I shall have time enough to suffer!

But I must relate to you what has taken place here.

On reaching the terminus of their journey, during which, as you are aware, they pretended not to know each other, my friends separated. Dumont accompanied Kiusko to his castle, which is situated two leagues from Kichenau; Giraud, Jacquet, and Joseph took up their abode in a little-frequented hotel of the town, so as to search the neighborhood, according to any indications Dumont could give them as to Kondjé-Gul's discovery.

For two months all search was vain, when, one day, Dumont's suspicions were awakened as to that relative of Kiusko, whom none of his friends knew, and who was hardly ever seen in the castle. When questioned concerning her, Kiusko had answered that she was a foreigner, who had experienced reverses of fortune, and

to whom he had offered a'home. This fact, reported to
Giraud, started him on the scent (the woman had arrived
at the castle just a month before the day Kiusko quitted
Paris). Joseph alone knew Madame Murrah and Kondjé-
Gul, as he had followed them during the time he had
been employed by the Pole. That is why Giraud took
him on the journey. So Dumont, one morning, brought
Joseph to the castle as his servant; he had need of a
man, he said, to help him in his mineralogical excursions.
His meeting with a Frenchman in Russian Bessarabia.
explained his choice in a very plausible fashion, and the
count saw nothing suspicious in it. At the end of three
days, Joseph managed to catch sight of the Circassian;
he recognized her as she was getting into a carriage, and
jumped up behind without being perceived by the coachman. After a two-hours' drive the carriage stopped in X,
at the door of a Greek convent. He immediately
informed Giraud, who went the next day into the country,
and, aided by a gypsy, who served him as a guide, he
succeeded in discovering that the woman in question
came once a week to visit her daughter at the convent.
He then sent for me.

We have arranged together, taking into consideration
what they know of the country, a plan, which we shall
begin to execute to-morrow. We are going to leave
Khorestakh. Although we live very retired, the presence
of four strangers may attract attention, and, beside, we
are too far from X, whence we shall try to carry
off Kondjé-Gul. In the neighborhood of the convent is
a village of Hungarian gypsies, where Yanos, Giraud's
guide, lives. I shall buy up the whole tribe if necessary,
and we are to live hidden among them until we have
everything prepared.

CHAPTER XL.

I have had a letter from Kondjé-Gul! She calls me, implores me to rescue her. She loves me always! The trembling hand in which I have written these last words will show you how much I have suffered! Well, yes! in the delirium of my bitter despair, this thought tortured me. Throwing aside my faith in her, forgetting the loyalty of her heart, worn out by my sorrow, I have at times almost doubted her. But she loves me still; she appeals to me, as eager to see me as I am to see her!

But I am forgetting to tell you about it.

The day after I wrote you my last letter, we quitted Khorestakh. Yanos had prepared for us a shelter in his tribe, after having consulted the chief and the council. Thanks to our being foreigners, we were received with confidence. The arrival of Dumont, who soon joined us, changed toleration into real hospitality. He traveled once in Hungary, and he speaks Romany a little. As he is a Freemason, and as this fact has often been of service to him, it occurred to him to see if there were any brother Masons among the gypsies. The next day he found that the chief of the tribe, himself, was a member of the order, and he made himself known to him as a grand-master. A meeting of the lodge, at which half the men of the village were present, was held to receive and honor him with Masonic rites. From that moment he and his friends were sacred. We could live there, therefore, certain of not being discovered, in the midst of the tribe, and we set to work. Dumont declared that we were all engineers come to explore the country which gave an excuse for our excursions. Three or four young gypsies, brave and determined, including Yanos, have been enrolled as our guides; the desire for gain will induce them to serve us in the most active fashion when the time comes. Yanos, who is half in our confidence, assures us, beside, of their good will.

This result obtained, the first important point was to communicate with Kondjé-Gul. This is how we managed it:

The Greek convent where she is confined is a branch of the important monastery of Rézina. Built in a barren ravine, it is backed by enormous rocks, which almost overhang the building, itself hidden to the roof by the walls inclosing it. Two or three rather perilous excursions enabled us to get an idea of the surroundings. With what science we possess among us, we can surmount all difficulties. However, it was absolutely necessary to let Kondjé-Gul know of our presence. We passed nearly ten days in vainly striving to obtain information as to what part of the convent she was in, without succeeding in the least. All that we could learn was that the Greek convents are divided into two parts, one of which is devoted to the nuns, and the other to neophytes of a lower rank, who fill the office of servants, and can come out when they choose. Through one of the latter it would be possible to open communication. Fortunately Yanos spoke to us of a young gypsy girl, employed in the convent, where a priest, believing her to be half converted, had obtained a place for her. Three days afterward I saw the young gypsy. She could give us only the vaguest details. Kondjé-Gul appeared to be the object of particular care and of a stricter surveillance than the nuns, from whom she was, so to speak, sepa-

15

rated, never walking with them in the garden. The girl assured me, however, that she could reach her and speak to her in private. I then wrote to Kondjé-Gul the following words on a fly-leaf of the prayer-book the gypsy girl carried, with the advice'to destroy them as soon as she had read them: "I am here. Confide in the one who brings you this."

Two days after, I received an answer from Kondjé-Gul, written on another fly-leaf. The gypsy, this time took back, hidden in her dress, some writing-paper and a pencil. I asked Kondjé-Gul to give me all the details necessary to effect her escape. The next day but one, the gypsy brought me this letter:

"André, André, you live! You are near me! You love me still! They have deceived me. I thought myself lost. I longed to die, and you have come to save me! When I read those dear words of yours, which informed me of your presence and told me to confide in your messenger, I almost fainted from joy. For an instant I doubted the evidence of my senses; I thought I was going mad, and that I was the victim of a hallucination. Then I feared some snare. My impulse was to fly from the garden and shut myself up in my prison, hide myself behind the walls where no one could hear my cries. But my eyes recognized your dear handwriting.

"And you? How you must have suffered! But I must answer what you require; you must know what they have done, so that you can foil their plans and deliver me.

"You remember that last day of our happy life. Fanny told me that you had come in the morning, and that you had talked for a very long time with my mother. This

worried me; you had gone away without coming to
see me; but I expected you to dinner, and I resolved
not to go out in order not to lose a moment of your
beloved presence, in case you should come early. At
six o'clock, my mother entered my room, apparently
in great trouble; she held in her hand a dispatch
signed with your name, which she had just received,
she said, and in which you informed her that you
had fought with Count Kiusko. You were wounded,
dying, and you asked for me. The dispatch was
dated from the place where the duel had occurred,
Meaux. I dressed myself, wild with anxiety, to hasten
to join you. We went to the station and took a train.
How could I conceive of any deception? Two men,
whom, from some words they let fall, I concluded to be
physicians, were in the carriage with us. I questioned
them; they told me it would take two hours to reach
you. I glued my face to the window, longing to anni-
hilate space, and watched the names of the stations,
when, suddenly, as we approached a town, I read afar
off distinctly, ' Meaux.'

"I rose to be ready to get out; but scarcely was I on
my feet, when we reached the station. The train passed
it at full speed. I uttered a cry, thinking there was some
mistake. I tried to open the door, resolved to leap out
of the carriage. They seized me; I tried to release myself, but I was no match for their strength. I implored
and wept. Then my mother told me the truth. They
were carrying me away from you. I learned who the two
men were; one, an emissary of our embassy, and the
other a French agent of police, both summoned by my
mother to force me to follow her.

"At this revelation, I knew no more what happened.

It seemed to me that my heart stopped beating, and I
lost all consciousness.

"When I came to myself it was night; I was still in the
same carriage, which was faintly lighted; I knew that
long hours must have passed, during which you had
been expecting me, dying, cursing me, perhaps. I again
implored my mother, begging her on my knees to take
me to you. In the midst of my sobs, I swore to her
that I would submit and follow her, as soon as you were
out of danger. One of the men, moved to pity, said a
few words to her in a low tone; but icy and inexorable,
she replied by a gesture of refusal. The night passed;
in the morning, we arrived at a city, which I learned
was Strasburg. I thought that, at least, I could find
means of writing to you; but they took me to a private
room until another train should be ready to start.
As I was lying, motionless and worn out, upon a sofa,
one of the men who had accompanied us bent over me,
while my mother was speaking to the other, and said
rapidly: "Be comforted, you have been deceived; Monsieur de Peyrade is alive; he has not fought." Almost
before he had finished speaking, my mother made me get
up. There was another man there, who had been waiting for us; we entered a reserved compartment with him,
and the train started.

"I knew now that my mother would be implacable, and
that I had nothing more to hope for. I thought only of
watching for an opportunity of writing to you. You lived,
and my energy returned. My thoughts were directed
to but one end: To fly, to hide myself, to summon you,
or return to you myself. Suddenly a horrible suspicion
seized me. Suppose that man's words of consolation
were untrue; suppose he had deceived me to give me

hope so that I would be more resigned! I fought against this torturing doubt all day and all night, and, finally, I begged my mother to tell me the truth; she said that the dispatch was true, and that the man had lied to me out of pity.

" On the third day, we reached Pesth. There she made me embark on a Danube boat. I did not know where they were taking me. Shut up in a cabin, I could communicate with none of the passengers. This lasted for eight days. The man whom we met at Strasburg was always with us. Then we landed and took another train; finally, one evening, we alighted at a station where a carriage was in waiting, and a few hours afterward we arrived at the convent where I now am. My mother left me, utterly prostrated, with no hope even of knowing your fate. Two weeks later, she came to see me, and for the first time since we left Paris, told me where I was. She then revealed to me her wishes and resolve. My marriage with Count Kiusko was decided upon. I was not to leave my prison until the day I should be his wife. I had already guessed their miserable plot. I did not forget you, and I declared to her that, dead or living, I was yours, and that my first act of liberty would be to kill myself to escape from their violence.

" Since that day, she has come once a week, counting on my weakness or despair; but I love you, and my life is yours. One day they told me that I was to be made a Christian. This was your religion; I embraced it, and I have placed my confidence in your God. My heart grew lighter, and under the indignities to which I am subjected I have found in your faith the strength to resist their threats, and to so conduct myself that I may live with you through all eternity in your heaven.

"André, dear André, I love you, I love you! Save me if you can; but, I implore you, do not expose your life. Living or dead, I belong to you; I am your wife, and, by *our* God, I promise never to be any one's but yours."

Louis, after reading this letter, the prayers I had lisped as a child returned to my lips.

CHAPTER XLI.

With Kondjé-Gul ready to second us, our enterprise now required nothing but audacity; but we had to trust something to chance. A defeat would ruin all my hopes; it was necessary to succeed in our first attempt, or else, the alarm given, we were lost.

We set to work, aided this time by precise information from Kondjé-Gul. In order to confine her as closely as possible, and to isolate her from the nuns, who in Greek convents enjoy a considerable amount of liberty, they had placed her in a remote cell, used as a sort of place of punishment. This cell, situated at the back of the convent, was lighted by a solitary window opening upon a deep ravine, the opposite side of which is formed by an immense rock, towering one hundred and fifty feet above the convent buildings, which are considered to be inaccessible from that side. From information given us by the gypsy girl, we soon had a plan of the convent gardens and inclosure. A sort of quadrilateral of high walls, and difficult to scale, incloses the whole convent. But this would be no obstacle for us; the place is isolated, and should we be obliged to accomplish Kondjé-Gul's rescue by main force, success was possible; but the alarm of such an attempt would spread in an instant, and we should be pursued and overtaken before we could reach

Odessa, where I had sent Giraud to hire a vessel at any cost. From Odessa, we could reach the coast of Asia.

All the chances calculated, we resolved to have recourse to the boldest means of all, and the one which apparently was the least possible of execution. This was to attempt her abduction from the ravine side of the convent, which no one would think of watching.

To give no chance for suspicion, Dumont had commenced serious operations in the neighborhood. It was known that, aided by five or six gypsies, he had sunk several shafts and blasted one or two granite rocks to lay bare the ore. Our plan formed, he announced that it was his intention to explore a deep gorge, into which it was possible to descend only by means of a basket attached to ropes and pulleys. This machine was ordered of a carpenter in the town, from designs made by ourselves, and adapted to the form of the precipice where we really intended to use it. The work would require eight days. We waited, and finally it arrived one evening when Dumont was making a call at Kiusko's castle.

In his absence, I gave the orders, and told our men to be on foot early in the morning. We had resolved to first make a descent into the ravine some distance from the convent, to see that all was right, and to render our gypsies familiar with the use of the ropes and pulleys. These measures arranged, we decided that our expedition to the convent should take place the next night but one.

Matters were in this state when Yanos arrived. He brought me the following lines from Kondjé-Gul, sent in haste by the gypsy girl who served as our messenger.

"The priest has come to prepare me for this horrible news; they intend to force me to obey their wishes, and

my mother will come to-morrow to remove me from the convent."

When I read this, I was filled with consternation. All was lost if we did not act that very night. Dumont returned, as we were discussing the situation. Certain preparations at Kiusko's castle had given him the alarm.

In an instant, all our plans were changed. Yanos hastened through the village to awaken our men. Fortunately, during the days we were obliged to wait, we had calculated everything and made all our arrangements. A wagon had been hired the day before to carry the basket and pulleys. An hour later, men and horses were ready, and we set out. The night was dark; but we had so often traversed the path that we knew every foot of it. It was nearly midnight when we reached the rocky platform overlooking the convent. There we had to await the arrival of the wagon, which had been forced to come by another and longer road. Armed with pickaxes, we did the work necessary for fastening the pulleys. I was terribly agitated, but the resolute coolness of Dumont, Giraud, and Jacquet sufficed to accomplish the task. Finally, at two o'clock, all was in readiness. The basket in which I was to make the descent hung suspended over the abyss. Giraud wished to test it by means of a block of granite; but as that would take time, I opposed it, and, without listening to him, I seized the ropes and took my place.

At a signal given by Dumont, the men commenced to lower the basket, and I descended into the shadows of the ravine, the darkness of which grew blacker and blacker as I went down. For some time, balanced in space, I had all I could do to preserve myself from the jagged points of the rock. Below me, I could see the window of the cell, where Kondjé-Gul must be sleeping. Although I had had no time to warn her, I hoped to be able to awaken her without noise. She would doubtless be upon her guard, as she knew all about our plan. Suddenly a frightful thought seized me. Suppose she were not there? Perhaps on this last night which she was to remain a captive, they had transferred her to another part of the convent. All these thoughts, in the midst of my danger, assailed me at once. Finally, I arrived at the top of the window. A little cord, hanging by my side, and the end of which Giraud held in his hand, was to serve me to give, by a certain number of pulls, information in case I should encounter any unforeseen obstacle. I gave the signal to stop lowering, and it was obeyed. We had calculated minutely the space between me and the window, when I should be on a level with it. The basket hung about four feet from the walls of the convent. By means of a pole provided with hooks, with which I was furnished, I seized the bar across the window, and drew myself toward it; then I tied my basket securely to the bar. This done, I was about to tap on the glass, when the window opened. Kondjé-Gul was awake and had heard the noise. I heard a stifled cry, and then these words:

"André! My André! Is it you?"

I leaped into the chamber, and she threw herself in my arms; but our moments were precious.

"Come! Come!" I whispered.

In less time than it takes to describe it, I had placed her in the basket and stepped in beside her. The very sight of her had made another man of me. While I unknotted the rope, she held us steady by the bar, for fear that some sudden oscillation should dash us against the rock

opposite and we should both be thrown out by the
shock.   Then, seizing my pole, I gently eased the basket
off, and gave the signal to draw us up.   The ropes
tightened, and we commenced our ascent.   But the
danger, which I had not thought of before in my feverish
haste, now frightened me.   I could feel the quick beating of Kondjé-Gul's heart.   We scarcely dared to speak;
our voices had a strange sound, and the darkness was so
intense that we could barely distinguish each other's
faces.   A night-bird, disturbed by the singular visitors
who had troubled its solitude, flew about our heads,
screaming and flapping its wings.   Kondjé-Gul made an
involuntary movement of alarm, which caused the basket to swing from side to side.

"Have no fear!" I said, quickly.

"What matters it?" she answered.   "I shall die with
you!"

Finally we reached the top; Jacquet was in readiness,
and seizing the basket, he drew it onto the platform.

We were saved!

In a few moments we had torn up the pulleys.   This
was necessary in order that they should not be perceived
the next morning from the windows of the convent,
which would betray all.   It was probable that when they
entered the cell, not finding her there, their first thought
would be that in despair she had committed suicide.   Her
window, which I had purposely left open, would lead
them to believe that she had thrown herself into the
ravine.

Our last precautions taken, and the basket and ropes
hidden away, we hastened along the path which led to
the village.   The greatest dispatch was necessary.   It
was now three o'clock in the morning, and we had only

a few hours of darkness before us. A boy's dress had
been prepared for Kondjé-Gul, and while she was changing her garments, horses, selected by a gypsy horse-
jockey, were saddled. Half an hour afterward, we were
galloping along the road, Kondjé-Gul seated behind me
with her arms around my waist. Of all the brave gypsy
boys who had aided us, Yanos alone accompanied us as
guide, for, in order to reach Odessa, we might be forced
to leave the highways, in case we were pursued, and hide
in some gypsy village.

It would take us nearly two hours to reach the first
town, where, at a little inn, we should find a carriage.
The horse-jockey had left early in the evening to make
arrangements for changes of horses as far as Tiraspol.
When day broke, we had gone about eight leagues, and
we soon reached the village. We were expected; breakfast was served, and we halted for half an hour.

My poor Kondjé-Gul was worn out, but our happiness
cast us both into a sort of delirium. Giraud, Dumont,
and Jacquet, enthusiastic at our success, indulged in all
sorts of pranks. But poor Joseph, who had never before
mounted a horse in his life, and whom we had been
obliged to tie into his saddle, was glum enough.

However, these few moments of repose did not make
us forget our danger. A few words of Kondjé-Gul's
startled us. They had matins at the convent at five
o'clock. At that hour, they must have discovered her
disappearance. Kiusko would be immediately informed,
and we had only two-hours' start of him in our flight,
but, should he be accompanied by his friends, we were
well armed and determined to defend ourselves.

We started off again in a great stage-coach, drawn by
eight shaggy, little horses, the leaders ridden by two

postilions, of whom Yanos was one.   We went at head-
long speed, but we encountered very bad roads.   About
the middle of the day we reached Baschloï.

CHAPTER XLII.

There are certain supreme moments which are entirely
in the hands of chance, when the least grain of sand may
destroy all human previsions.   We had left Baschloï and
were descending, almost at a gallop, the steep declivity
of the hill, when, all at once, at a turn in the road, Yanos
appeared to us to be making strenuous efforts to rein in
his horses.

"Are they running away?" I called out.

"No! no!   It is not that," he answered, "but I must
stop them."

After a few minutes, he succeeded in slackening our
pace, and leaped from the saddle.

The box of one of our wheels was on fire.

We all descended, and Jacquet, Giraud, and Joseph
ran off in different directions to try and discover a spring
of water.   Meanwhile we attempted to stay the progress
of the fire with sand, but the box was in a blaze, and
before we knew it, it cracked and the wheel fell to
pieces.

It was impossible to continue our journey.   Our only
resource was to return to Baschloï and procure another
vehicle.   The postilion took one of the horses and
departed.   We should have to wait more than an hour
for his return, and I felt that this delay might ruin us.

I questioned Yanos as to the danger we ran of being
overtaken.

"Well," he responded, "if the count left two hours after us in a carriage, his horses will never catch up with ours."

"But suppose he is on horseback?" I asked.

"Oh! in that case," he replied," by roads which I know, he could be in Tiraspol before you."

It was imprudent to remain in the road; passers-by might notice us, and be able to give precise information, if they should be encountered by our pursuers. So we entered a thicket, bordering on the road, leaving Yanos to watch for the return of his companion. Joseph had discovered a brook, and Kondjé-Gul bathed her burning forehead.

This unfortunate accident had thrown us all into consternation, and we did not dare to speak to each other of our fears, as the same presentiment of evil weighed upon us all. Our gaiety had disappeared, and we all waited in the deepest anxiety.

Suddenly Giraud, who had mounted guard on a rock, uttered a cry of joy.

"There is our postilion!" he exclaimed.

I joined him, and I saw, but still some distance off, a man on horseback galloping along the road. Just as I was joyfully confirming this good news to my friends, I heard Yanos calling me: "Quick! quick! take your precautions!" he whispered to me, when I approached him. "My eyes are better than yours. That is not Zafi, but Count Daniel. I know him from his black mare, which my father sold him."

"What shall we do?" I said.

"Hide, and hope that he will pass, without stopping, an abandoned carriage."

As he said these words, he took his horse by the bridle, and, leading him to the wood where we had taken

shelter, tied him to a tree.   Ten minutes of the greatest
anxiety passed.   The horseman was rapidly approaching.
He was soon near enough to distinguish his features.   It
was indeed   Kiusko.   Lying flat on the grass, and
hidden in the bushes, we watched him.   He perceived the
carriage, and we saw him rein in his horse.   When he
came up to it, he stopped and glanced about him.

However he seemed to look upon it simply as an
accident to some travelers, who had reached the next
village on foot, and he was about to ride on, when our
horse, tied ten feet behind us, neighed to the mare.
Daniel raised his head.   We saw his look fixed upon the
freshly-trampled grass.   He turned his horse toward us.

We were discovered.

With a bound I rose to my feet, and he recognized me.
For a moment, a mad thought took possession of my
brain.   He was there, face to face, and—but I remembered Kondjé-Gul.   To render her a witness of a combat between us would perhaps kill her.   However, we
both were armed, and the situation was desperate.   Blind
with rage, I advanced toward him, when I heard these
words, quickly spoken by Yanos to Dumont.

"Will you authorize me?"

"Yes," replied Dumont.

I heard a report, and saw Kiusko turn in his saddle
and fall to the ground.

"What have you done?" I cried.

And I hastened to the aid of the wounded man.

One of his feet was caught in the stirrup and I dis-
engaged it.   But as I seized his frightened horse by the
bridle to prevent her from trampling upon him, Giraud
called out:

"Take care!"

I turned; Kiusko, in a sitting posture, with his right arm hanging inert, had drawn with his left hand a pistol, which he was cocking with his teeth; then, rapidly, as all rushed at him, he aimed it at Kondjé-Gul and fired almost instantaneously.

Kondjé-Gul's hat fell off. I uttered a cry of fury. I heard a second, then a third report, but Jacquet had thrown himself upon Kiusko, and knocked his arm up into the air.

"Are you wounded?" I cried.

"No," she replied.

All this passed like a flash.

Kiusko, held by Jacquet's iron strength, yelled like a wild beast; but, once disarmed, there was nothing more to fear from him. After the danger Kondjé-Gul had run, I no longer felt any pity.

"You know that you can find me, when it suits your convenience," I said to him.

He answered only by blasphemies and a look of furious hate; but his wound was bleeding, and his frantic struggles had taken away his strength. A ghastly pallor overspread his face.

"We are bound to show him common humanity," said Dumont, shrugging his shoulders. "To work, Jacquet, but make haste, for I hear the carriage, and monsieur, who appears to have no prejudices against killing women, will perfectly understand that we are in a hurry to remove mademoiselle as far from him as possible."

Jacquet had already produced his case of instruments; in an instant, Kiusko's garments were cut open and the wound laid bare. The ball, which had struck him full in the breast, had fortunately glanced aside. The right collar-bone was broken.

"That is nothing," said Jacquet; "it will only lay him up for a month. The wound is not a bad one; I can feel the ball at the end of my probe. In a quarter of an hour I shall have finished with him."

During the operation Kiusko fainted.

"So!" said Dumont. "There is a little of the chicken in this noble boyar, he can not stand pain."

We now had to decide what to do. Kiusko, although wounded, could still stop our flight, denounce us to the police, put them on our tracks, and have us arrested before we could reach Tiraspol. However, it was impossible to leave him without aid in his condition. We consulted, and Yanos relieved us from our embarrassment.

"Monsieur Dumont," he said, "you authorized the accident, did you not? I can not remain without danger in this country."

"Yes, I will take you with me," I replied, quickly; "I will take charge of you."

"Well, then," continued Yanos, "this is my advice. We will leave the man who has brought the carriage here. While he remains with the count, let Zafi go to one of our villages and bring back some trusty friends. They will carry away the wounded man and keep him till to-morrow. To-night, by means of the railway from Tiraspol, we shall have time to reach Odessa. By the time Count Daniel can act we shall be at sea."

This plan was an admirable one, and Yanos called Zafi and gave him his instructions. Meanwhile, Jacquet had finished his operation. The gypsy postilion was told what he was to do, and we entered the carriage and drove rapidly away toward Tiraspol. At midnight we embarked at Odessa.

CHAPTER XLIII.

The ship chartered by Giraud was a Greek vessel of good size and well appointed. She was called the "Eudoxie." This, being my aunt's name, seemed to me to be a good omen. The crew was composed of fifteen men. The captain, whom Jacquet dubbed upon the spot *Canaris*, was one of those old experienced sea-dogs, who could pilot a vessel himself in any of the ports as far as Marseilles. We were out of reach of all pursuit free from all fear, and the sea before us.

I will not attempt to describe to you our boisterous spirits. Free from all troubles, we could scarcely believe we had ever experienced any. My poor Kondjé-Gul, still pale from the hardships and sorrows she had undergone, beamed with happiness, and contemplated me as if she could not believe her eyes. What delight it was to speak of our past griefs, regrets, and despair! Hand in hand, we both talked at the same time, the same words came to our lips, and the same hymn of thanksgiving welled up in our hearts!

It was splendid weather; it almost seemed as if the heavens were rejoicing at her deliverance. We were soon in sight of the coast of Asia. Seated in the cabin, with my arms about her, she told me of all her childish privations and her thoughts, when, as a young girl, she wandered, almost in rags, in the gardens of the *Sweet Waters.*

We passed Constantinople under full sail, and we stopped for only one day at Athens. I bought some clothes there for Kondjé-Gul and I parted with my

16

friends. Despite the fraternal affection which will always bind us together, they felt that just now they were *de trop*. I left Joseph and Yanos with them. The next day, the "Eudoxie" weighed anchor, bearing away *us two*.

How can I describe our voyage? Happiness has no history, as I wrote you when beginning this recital. Poor me! I thought myself happy then! with my eyes gazing into Kondjé-Gul's. If you only knew how am converted!

After a most favorable voyage, we came in sight of Toulon in a terrible storm. One would have said that the tempest had come to recall to our memory that the future was threatening. In fact, for the three weeks since we left Odessa, disappearing suddenly without leaving any trace, I had given myself up to the happiness which we both felt at being united again after so many days of anguish and alarm. Confident in the absolute security of the sea, beyond reach of all attack, we had thought only of our present happiness, our love, and our tenderness. And if sometimes a vague fear of what fate might have in store for me would come to me, I would drive it hastily away. However, it was now necessary for me to face reality. What safe retreat could I choose to hide Kondjé-Gul in, from the search which her mother had doubtless already begun? Kiusko knew of our flight, his bitter enmity still continued, and I must expect to suffer from his vengeance and his jealous passion, excited almost to madness. In any place, the Circassian, supported and counseled by him, could seize her daughter, claim her by the simplest appeal to the law, and no human power could set at naught her rights. Our present happiness could last only till the day when, forced to appear among my own family, my

very presence would oetray a.., and set on foot investi-
gations which would infallibly end in her discovery.
Suppose their plans were already laid? The Circassian and Kiusko must have been in Paris for the last
twenty days; suppose they should be lying in wait for
us? The " Eudoxie " must already be signaled by the
officers of the port; she came from Odessa; might they
not conjecture, taking into consideration the day and
hour of her departure, that we were on board? Perhaps
orders had already been given to arrest us the very
moment we set foot on shore.

These reflections caused me the greatest alarm. I
thought of putting out to sea again. But might not our
description have been sent to all the ports? Were not the
violation of a convent, the abduction of a young girl
placed there by her mother, crimes for which a warrant
could easily be obtained in whatever place we might be
found?

All these thoughts flashed one after the other through
my brain, and, taken by surprise in my senseless freedom
from anxiety, I was for a moment almost overwhelmed
by them. Kondjé·Gul was by my side, confident and
happy, contemplating the shores of France.

"André," she said, "a little over a year ago, from these
very waters, I gazed upon the unknown land, to which I
was being brought as a slave. How much has happened
since then!" "Good-morning, my country!" she cried,
in a transport of love and joy.

. And, putting her hands to her lips, she threw kisses
toward the shore. She thought herself saved, and I
concealed from her my anxiety.

But I must at least try to escape from the ambush
into which it was almost certain we were about foolishly

to fall. Consc.ous of danger, I immediately resolved not to land in France. To take Kondjé-Gul to Férouzat, as was my first idea, would perhaps ruin us both. It was too probable that it would be suspected we should choose that refuge, for us to risk appearing there.

My plan decided upon, I ordered the captain to continue our voyage, as if our destination were Marseilles; then, when out of sight of land, I told him to direct his course toward the coast of Italy. When night came, we were off Oneglia. Fortunately, the storm had abated, and we could be rowed ashore. • About midnight the ship stopped near a fishermen's village. We lowered a boat and in ten minutes we were on land. I took leave of my good captain, who could not have been entirely ignorant of our situation. The " Eudoxie " was, moreover, at my disposition for three months. It was arranged that he should sail, as if bound for Barcelona, showing himself at all ports, so as to be signaled. He will then go to Marseilles, having on board only his crew, and will say that he landed us on the coast of Spain, if, by chance, he is questioned.

Kondjé-Gul had suspected, from the change in our plans, that I feared some misfortune. I reassured her by saying that Férouzat was in no state to receive us, and that we were going to remain some days in Italy, until it could be made in readiness.

We passed through the little fishing village. It would have been imprudent to awaken the people, as that would have shown we had just come on shore; so we walked to Oneglia, reaching there about daybreak. It is from Oneglia that I am now writing you.

CHAPTER XLIV.

I had feared perils, my dear Louis; but they have surpassed my worst forebodings. My happiness, my life, Kondjé-Gul's fate and mine, are no longer but a question of hours, and the most horrible catastrophe is imminent.

On my arrival at Oneglia, I wrote to my uncle. He alone could aid me, and I begged him to come to me. He was in total ignorance of my position, and the gravity of the circumstances would perhaps make it absolutely necessary for me to confide in him. To justify my abrupt departure from Paris, I had invented a pretext of a journey to Hungary, where I was going, I said, to hunt for a few weeks with a friend. My letters, since then, had told him nothing, except that, through caprice, we had pushed on into Bessarabia. A few lines from Athens, finally, had announced to him my return. I trembled at the thought of the anger he would feel, when I was forced to reveal to him my expedition and its consequences.

I have seen him again; my father, my great, good, noble, and brave friend, and he has pardoned all, despite the wrong I have done him.

Last evening, after an uneasy day, during which I had not been able to conceal my anxiety from Kondjé-Gul, we took a walk to a hill, from which can be seen the road to Nice. We walked along, she leaning on my arm and gently questioning me as to an annoyance which she felt, she said, when, as we reached a turn in the path, a man, approaching with a rapid step, suddenly appeared before us. It was my uncle. He had left his carriage to take a short-cut to Oneglia. I had no sooner recognized him, than, without reflection, I ran toward him, thinking only of my delight at seeing him; he opened his arms, and pressed me to his heart like a prodigal son.

"My boy!" he cried. "What has happened?"

But, at this moment, he perceived Kondjé-Gul, standing timidly a few steps off and not daring to approach.

"Ah! I understand all!" he added. "It is she! You have been to seek her!"

And, without any reproachful word, he advanced and held out his hand to her, as at Paris. Poor Kondjé-Gul's emotion was so vivid, that she trembled like a leaf.

"Why, what is she afraid of now?" said my uncle. "But, children that you are, why did you not tell me all?"

We went to a little house, which I had hired in the town. My uncle was hungry, and Kondjé-Gul herself got him some supper. Divining that I did not wish to speak before her, he asked me no questions, nor did he say anything of what he knew already. Finally, we were alone.

"Well," he said, "you are in a fine fix. Someone came to the hôtel, two weeks ago, to question me as to an alleged attempt at assassination upon the highway."

"An assassination?" I cried.

"It is exactly as I have the honor to repeat it to you. But we will return to that later. Now tell me this whole affair."

I then related to him faithfully all that you know, revealing to him first who Kondjé-Gul was, and how I had separated her from my harem and placed her in a pension.

" I ought to have suspected it," he exclaimed, striking his forehead.

I then told of my rivalry with Kiusko, his intrigues with the Circassian, and their violence to Kondjé-Gul, who was deceived by a false dispatch from me announcing that I had been grievously wounded in a duel.

"Ah, but that Daniel is a rascal!" exclaimed my uncle, when I came to this. "But go on, pass over your heart-ache and come to the matter which troubles you now."

I informed him of my active search with the aid of Dumont, Jacquet, and Giraud, who had followed Daniel to Bessarabia; of the discovery of Kondjé-Gul, my journey, and our attempt at her rescue, which had so miraculously succeeded. Then of the encounter with Kiusko, wounded by Yanos, and left in the hands of the gypsies, while we fled to Tiraspol and Odessa.

"Whew! All that was not badly managed," he said, when I had finished. "But, once more, what the devil made you tell me nothing about it?"

"But, uncle," I said, touched at this great-hearted indulgence, which spared me even the slightest reproach, "what could I do?"

"What could you do? What could you do?" he replied. "Why, you had only to put the whole affair in my hands! I would have had it executed by five or six of my sailors, and you would have come out of it white as snow, spending your time at the club, and then I should never have missed you at the whist-table. That is what you could have done! But there is no use in talking about that now; the folly has been committed, and the thing now is to get you out of your scrape. What have you determined upon? Have you arranged any plan?"

" None, uncle," I answered, sadly. " I have thought

only of preserving Kondjé-Gul from being discovered and taken away by her mother, and, in my ignorance of all the rest, I wrote to you for your advice."

"Humph! the rest is very simple. Your aunt, who has relations in the Russian embassy, has been informed, in confidence, that your extradition has been demanded. And if Kiusko brings you to trial "ou may expect the worst."

"What?" I cried, " This accusation   assassination serious?"

" Nothing could be more serious,   said my uncle, "and it is an offense of common law sufficient for the Russian government to have you arrested anywhere. So, you see, you must be securely hidden as soon as possible."

I was stricken with consternation at this new complication, which I had not foreseen. In fact, Kiusko, set at liberty by the gypsies, could not have failed to make a complaint and accuse us, were it only to try and stop our flight and seize Kondjé-Gul again, before we should have succeeded in reaching Odessa. Must not the men left with him and who had carried him away, have given their testimony as witnesses, for fear of being compromised? I was, despite all, an accomplice in the attempt on his life, and nothing could save me from an accusation, which he would doubtless pursue with rage, to assure my ruin and deliver him from me. I was lost!

"Come," continued my uncle, "this is no time to regret your awkwardness. The first thing to do is to quit this place and return to France. The treaties do not permit governments to arrest our countrymen on our own soil for crimes committed abroad. Here, you being a Frenchman is sufficient for the Russian ambassador to have you arrested by the Italian police; we must, there-

fore, depart to-night. The "Belle-Virginie" was fortunately at Marseilles; so, on my way here, I gave orders to
Rabassu to come and join me at once at Oneglia. By
crowding on all steam, the ship should be in sight before
daylight. Rabassu will signal us and will send us a
boat to a spot on the shore he knows. To-morrow evening we will land at a place in the Camargue, from whence
you will go to Theodore's at Mas de St. Julien; you can
remain there in safety as long a time as it is necessary.
All this means that you must not ruin your digestion by
brooding over your misfortunes and troubles with a
dejected air! You must do me the kindness to pluck up
your spirits, eat and sleep well, while I steer your bark.
Love is very pretty, no doubt, but you must not let it
interfere with our arrangements, and in a year, you
must be ready to marry Anna!"

In listening to these words, in the presence of the
wonderful calmness of this powerful nature, of his perfect coolness, even in the midst of such trials, and of his
decision of character which recoiled before nothing, I
felt like a child. For the first time, perhaps, I understood what Barbassou-Pacha was, and I felt so surely protected that I passed suddenly from depression to confidence.

"Poor uncle," I said, taking his hand. "How much
annoyance I cause you!"

"Bah! I have had a good deal more in my life!" he
answered, without the least emotion. "You will make
amends to me for this some day. The important thing,
now, is to get you out of the mess you have so stupidly
gotten into."

"Could I have abandoned Kondjé-Gul to the suffering they were preparing for her?"

"Ta! ta! ta! You are over head and ears in love; that is clear. But I am not a rigorist, as you know—beside, it would do no good to lecture! Youth must have its way, and I would rather you would commit follies now than later. You have still a year before you to finish your bachelor's life. I certainly prefer to see you in love as you are, than with some minx of a *danseuse*. I could never understand that sort of affair. But, my dear boy, you understand that if, to arrange this business and stop all prosecution against you, it is necessary to give her up and to return her to her mother, you must not hesitate an instant."

"Return her to her mother!" I cried, in affright. "But that would be to deliver her to Kiusko! Uncle! That is to make her life one of despair and endless torture! It will kill her; it will kill me! For I love her so dearly I should die if I lost her!"

"Come! come!" exclaimed my uncle. "To talk of dying is folly. Now, seriously, my dear boy, you know that I have counted on you for quite another future, in which I have placed all my hopes, and which is the object of my life. The happiness of my children is what I have thought of, meditated about, resolved on through all. And when I touch the realization of my dream, shall a foolish love affair make it vanish like smoke? See here," he added in a tone so full of manly and trusting tenderness that I was touched by it, " you don't think of causing me that sorrow?"

"No, no, uncle!" I said. quickly, seizing the hand he held out to me, and carrying it to my lips. "No, no! I will never cause you that sorrow. I love you and venerate you as a father and a friend. My life, heart, and soul are yours, and I should despise myself, as a miserable ingrate, if I did not sacrifice anything in the world to give you the happiness you have longed for, of seeing your two children married. I am of your flesh and blood, uncle, and that is sufficient. But it is because I *am* of your flesh and blood that I love my poor Kondjé-Gul, and that I wish to defend her, and that I wish to save her from the frightful violence which her mother and Kiusko contemplate. Think of the existence in store for her; think of what she would suffer, of what I myself would suffer at the thought of her being his wife!"

"There! there! Be calm!" said my uncle, more moved than he cared to show. "I understand you; I passed through all that when I married your aunt Eudoxie. So, may the devil take me, if I don't do everything in the world to prevent their touching a hair of her head. She is a nice child, and if there is any means of saving her from her worthy mother, you can rely upon me to effect it. Only, you also are in danger, and you must reflect. Kiusko, enraged as he is, is a man to be feared. It is he who will put the officers on your track. If they take you before he has withdrawn his complaint, you will have, at least, to undergo a trial before the Russian tribunals."

I was about to make some answer, when suddenly the door opened, and Kondjé-Gul appeared, pale as death, with terror depicted on her face. She threw herself on her knees before my uncle.

"Monsieur! monsieur!" she gasped. "Give me up! Give me up! He must be saved!"

We thought they had already come to arrest me.

"No, no!" she continued quickly. "Fear nothing; but I was there and I have heard all. I know the danger you run, André. Monsieur, take me, give me up to my mother! André will not suffer! I shall want to kill myself; I shall kill myself, and that will be all! He will weep for me, but he will be consoled."

Her sobs prevented her from continuing.

"Hush! hush!" I cried. "Uncle, do not listen to her!"

My uncle, startled as myself, gazed at her in silence; his hands were bathed with her tears. "Noble girl!" he said, at last.

And raising her without an effort, he took her in his lap, holding her in his arms like a child, with her head resting on his shoulder.

"There! there! You foolish little girl; don't cry like that," said he, smoothing her hair with his hand.

"What, the devil! Must I arrange your affair also, and prevent you from being married against your will, if I can? It is very noble, what you wished to do for André, and I shall never forget it. Come, dry those tears! There, she is setting off again! And I, too! Heaven bless lovers with all their extravagances! Why, one would think this was a funeral!"

As he had been ordered, Rabassu arrived at Oneglia during the night, and two hours before dawn we embarked on the "Belle-Virginie." I had never seen my uncle on board one of his vessels before. I now understood Barbassou-Pacha, his strength and his calmness. Served by such devoted men, I comprehended that character which never permitted vulgar obstacles to interfere with any of his plans. With eight or ten ships and such sailors, my uncle is a power.

CHAPTER XLV.

I write to you from Mas de St. Julien, a sure place of refuge. This property in the Camargue, with an area of ten leagues, is under the stewardship of Theodore, a god-son of Barbassou-Pacha, to whom he bears an astonishing resemblance. Starting as cabin-boy, at ten years of age, on one of his god-father's ships, he had risen to the rank of mate, when, two years ago, he came here to take the direction of Mas, on the death of his mother. He is about the same age as myself, and once, during my college vacation, the captain sent for him to come to Férouzat to be my playmate. You can be sure he takes good care of me.

My uncle returned to Paris the day after our arrival here. A few days ago, by a private messenger, I received letters from my aunt and from him, which have already reassured me as to the more imminent dangers of my critical situation. My aunt, whose host of relations has placed her in contact with all the diplomacy of Europe, has succeeded in obtaining an abatement in the proceedings directed against me. She will go to Bessarabia, if necessary, to have the complaint withdrawn. "Meanwhile," she writes me, "they will let the matter drop; *but do not show yourself.*" As you may imagine, in all the steps she has taken, she has not said a word to any one of Kondjé-Gul. As I had supposed, the Circassian is in Paris. On her arrival there, she went at once to the Hôtel de Téral, accompanied by a person who questioned Fanny and the servants. They do not know a word since my departure, so I have nothing to fear from their answers. My uncle, who informs me of these details, has seen a friend of the Turkish ambassador. Madame Murrah, he said, backed by great influence, has obtained from the French administration official aid in the search for her daughter. To stimulate their zeal, she scatters, with full hands, gold furnished by Kiusko's banker. The fight is a bitter one, as you see, and the least imprudence may ruin me. Do not write me, therefore, for fear of revealing my presence at Saint-Julien. Once upon my track, they could easily reach Kondjé-Gul, and I must be the principal object pointed out to all their spies.

My uncle, also inclosed me a letter from Giraud.

Thank heaven! These tried friends have returned and I need no longer tremble for them. Fortunately, Kiusko only knew Dumont among them, and he has denounced him to the authorities as well as myself. Yanos was unknown to him, and the gypsies who testified certainly did not betray him. Need I say whether I am attached to those noble hearts, who so generously devoted themselves to me, and whether I shall assist them in those difficulties of life, which weigh so heavily upon them and prevent the exercise of their rare faculties? You shall meet them all some day—Giraud, Dumont, and Jacquet.

CHAPTER XLVI.

A month has passed since we came to Mas, my dear Louis, and this strange romance of my life, of which you alone know all the exciting events, seems to me now like an incredible dream. It is only when I am at the height of my anxiety that I feel that it is all true, and that I am awake. It seems to me that I am walking in darkness;

lost in the depths of an abyss, and seeking an imaginary issue which I know does not exist. The brutal, inexorable fact is there, before me, and shuts out the future. Like the traveler who sees glide between his fingers the waters his parched lips long for, so, with my eyes fixed on Kondjé-Gul, I feel my hopes slipping away. To-morrow, perhaps, I say to myself, I shall see her no more. At this thought, my heart breaks! How can I save her, how dispute her with her mother, how defend her against the infamous designs of Kiusko? I believed, foolishly, in this happiness, free from all yoke of social conventions, and I perceive now the vanity of my dream, on awaking face to face with the realities of life.

My poor Kondjé-Gul strives to conceal from me her distress; but she knows all now, and the same cruel thought weighs upon us both. The future no longer exists for us, and from day to day we count the moments of our sad happiness. We sometimes anticipate the moment when we shall be discovered, when her mother shall come to seize her, to wrest her from me. And then, panting and distracted, straining me in her arms, to console my sorrow, she repeats to me her vow to die, to go and wait for me in heaven. Poor Kondjé-Gul, she is not yet nineteen! It is terrible!

CHAPTER XLVII.

Louis, it is all over! We have been discovered and surprised at Mas. You shall hear what has resulted from it.

I wrote you, two weeks ago, of the alarming information I had received as to the stubborn animosity of the

"This gentleman will tell you that such things are not done in his presence. Your daughter will remain with us to answer such questions as may be put to her. I offer her my arm, and if you will follow us, I shall have the honor of showing you the way."

Our hearts were in our throats, and Kondjé-Gul was trembling so that she could scarcely stand. We entered the house. My uncle, still perfectly calm, offered seats to Madame Murrah and the police officer; then he said, quietly:

"May I ask you, monsieur, if you are provided with a formal warrant, authorizing you to take mademoiselle away, according to her mother's desire?"

"I have an order from the judge!" cried Madame Murrah, vehemently.

"Oh! Pardon me! Pardon me!" said my uncle. "Pray let us keep our tempers. Will you, I beg, madame, allow monsieur to answer my question? We are anxious to observe the respect due to his office."

"Madame being a foreigner, monsieur," replied the officer, "as you seem to understand, my mission was simply to accompany her in order to draw up an official report, in case of opposition to her rights, so as to allow her to bring a suit before the courts."

"Ah!" ejaculated my uncle. "Well, monsieur, proceed, I beg, to take note of our declarations. In the first place, mademoiselle formally refuses to go with her mother."

"That is false!" exclaimed the Circassian. "She is my daughter, and she belongs to me. She will obey me, for she knows that I would curse her!"

"Let us be calm, and no useless words!" replied my uncle. "It is for your daughter to answer. Question her, monsieur."

The commissary turned to Kondjé-Gul and formulated his question. I saw her turn pale, hesitate, frozen with terror by her mother's look.

"Do you wish to leave me, then?" I said to her, with a throbbing heart.

"No! no!" she cried. Then, turning to the officer, she added in a resolute voice. "I do not wish to follow my mother, monsieur!"

At these words, the Circassian rose with a terrible glare in her eyes. Kondjé-Gul fell on her knees, imploring her forgiveness in despairing accents. In alarm, I rushed between them.

"Take her away!" said my uncle, quickly.

I raised her in my arms and carried her out of the room. At the door, I found Theodore and his sister, and I left her in their care.

Madame Murrah made a dash to follow her; but my uncle seized her by the wrist, and forced her to sit down again.

"Silence!" he said to her in Turkish. "We have not done yet, and if you budge, look out for yourself!"

"Officer!" cried the Circassian, "you see that he has used violence and threatened me!"

All this passed so rapidly that the commissary had had no time to interfere.

"Excuse me for having sent that child away, monsieur," said my uncle; "but you are, I think, already sufficiently edified as to her resolution. She is there, more-over, to answer you again, if you wish to interrogate her alone and free from all influence. It now remains for us to speak of what she must not hear. To her refusal to follow her mother, which she has just now so clearly expressed before you, will you add in your report that I also, on my part, refuse most emphatically to give her up?"

"You have no right to steal my daughter from me," cried the Circassian, almost insane with rage.

"That is what we are about to discuss," responded my uncle, tranquilly. "In the first place, monsieur, will you permit me to introduce myself to you, and to explain to you my position? My name is: The late Barbassou, formerly general and pacha in the service of His Majesty, the Sultan, which has given me the rights of a Turkish citizen."

The officer bowed in a way which showed that Barbassou-Pacha was known to him, as to everyone else.

"It results from these facts, monsieur," continued my uncle, "that the French courts have no jurisdiction over my private acts, and that this matter is one to be treated entirely between madame and myself. I will even add, expressing to you my regrets for the trouble it has caused you, that it was I, myself, who brought about this decisive interview. I went twice, in Paris, to call upon madame, desirous of putting an end to her demands. For reasons, which doubtless you can make a shrewd guess at, she refused to see me. I then arranged to have her daughter's presence at Mas de Saint-Julien made known to her, and I immediately came here, in order to have the pleasure of meeting her. There is the whole affair in a nutshell!"

"I refused to see you," exclaimed Kondjé-Gul's mother, "because I did not know you! And I demand to have my daughter returned to me; the sultan's ambassador claims her with me; I have his firman!"

Here the commissary intervened, and addressing my uncle, he said, gravely:

"Would you be kind enough, monsieur, to give your

reasons for refusing to surrender this young girl to her mother? You are probably not ignorant, that, according to our laws, in spite of the only semi-official character of the duty I am fulfilling, I am obliged to state them in my report."

"Certainly, monsieur," replied my uncle, "your request is a very proper one, and I will answer it as cheerfully as I should before the consul of His Excellency, the Turkish Ambassador, if madame had not serious reasons for avoiding, in his presence, this explanation between two Mussulman citizens, as both she and myself are."

"Please, continue, monsieur," replied the commissary, repressing a smile at this declaration of Barbassou-Pacha.

"Monsieur," proceeded my uncle, "I am a Turk and a Mohammedan, and according to the peculiar customs of my country, with which you are possibly acquainted, madame has given me her daughter, by a *bona fide*, serious contract, sanctioned by our usages, approved and guaranteed by our laws, which formally oblige me to protect her, to assure her always a position and a future in accordance with my fortune and condition in life. These laws also forbid me ever to abandon her. By this same contract, madame received a dowry, discussed, fixed, and consented to by herself. Before any Ottoman court, as you must see, monsieur, madame's claim would not be for a moment admitted and would be dismissed with scorn."

"We are in France," cried Madame Murrah, "and my daughter is free!"

"I will conclude my remarks, monsieur, said my uncle, without even noting that objection. "Madame and I are subjects of His Majesty, the Sultan. This whole matter is a contention between two citizens of the same nation, which can be brought before Turkish tribunals alone, and which your French jurisdiction, you understand, can take cognizance of, in no way whatever."

" You are not my daughter's husband!" screamed the Circassian. " She does not belong to you any longer, and our laws forbid all marriage with infidels!"

" Very true, madame," replied my uncle, " but you have made your daughter a Christian, in order to force her to marry Count Kiusko."

" But," he continued, interrupting himself, "these are details for private discussion, with which monsieur has nothing to do. And I think that he is now sufficiently well informed."

" Entirely so, monsieur," said the officer, rising. " I have taken note of your declaration, and my mission is fulfilled."

Barbassou-Pacha, at these words, saluted him in his most magnificent manner, and, with the greatest courtesy, ushered him out of the room.

The exasperated Circassian did not move. Rage was depicted on every feature, and she seemed determined to fight it out to the bitter end.

" He will have to let me speak to my daughter," she hissed, "and then we shall see!"

At this moment, my uncle re-entered, holding by the hand, Kondjé-Gul.

" Now, then, you old fool," said he, to Madame Murrah, suddenly changing his tone and manner, " you know now that you have nothing to do but to submit. Take back your silly words; you won't fare so badly after all. For I am going to marry your daughter to my nephew!"

I thought I had misunderstood him.

"Uncle!" I exclaimed. "What do you say?"

"You rascal! I must give her to you, since you adore each other like two idiots!"

Kondjé-Gul could not restrain a cry of joy. And we both threw ourselves at once into his arms.

"Yes," he said. "But it is all your aunt's doings! Ah! What has become of my famous projects?"

"Oh!" cried Kondjé-Gul, "we will love you so much!"

"All right, but don't strangle me! May heaven bless —— Well, yes," he continued, after a pause, embracing us both, "may heaven bless you, my children, and always give you happiness!"

Louis, my eyes were blinded with tears, but I would not dare to take my oath that, as he said these words, I did not see a pearly drop in the corner of Barbassou-Pacha's eye.

There are transports of happiness which can not be related. What more have I to say to you? We are all to go to Férouzat, where my aunt is expected in two days. Our marriage is to take place in three weeks. The Circassian, forced to consent to everything, departs, the day after the wedding, for that beautiful country of houris and pagan love, from which I have so happily returned.

Tell me, Louis, you who love, are you very sure that one has heart enough to love with a real love? That doubt makes me uneasy.

My compliments to your wife!

[THE END.]

Printed in the United Kingdom by
Lightning Source UK Ltd., Milton Keynes
138007UK00001B/49/A